1-99

THIS PLACE I KNOW

'...what do I know when I am in this place
that I can know nowhere else?'

Robert Macfarlane
The Old Ways.

THIS PLACE I KNOW
A NEW ANTHOLOGY OF CUMBRIAN POETRY

Editors
Kerry Darbishire
Kim Moore
Liz Nuttall

H
HANDSTAND PRESS

H
HANDSTAND PRESS

Published by Handstand Press.
East Banks, Dent, Sedbergh, Cumbria.
LA10 5QT.
www.handstandpress.net

First Published in 2018.

Designed and set by Russell Holden – Pixel Tweaks, Ulverston.
www.pixeltweakspublications.com

Cover illustration by Angie Mitchell
www.angiemitchell.co.uk

Printed in Poland for Latitude Press Limited.

ISBN: 978-0-9576609-6-0

FOREWORD

In June 1818, John Keats and his friend Charles Brown set off from Lancaster on a walking tour. Though bound for Scotland, they were keen to see the Lake District, and what they found far exceeded expectations. After taking the path up beside Stockghyll Force above Ambleside, Keats wrote ecstatically to his brother Tom:

> *What astonishes me more than any thing is the tone, the colouring, the slate, the stone, the moss, the rock-weed; or, if I may so say, the intellect, the countenance of such places. The space, the magnitude of mountains and waterfalls are well imagined before one sees them; but this countenance or intellectual tone must surpass every imagination and defy any remembrance. I shall learn poetry here and shall henceforth write more than ever...*

Keats's letter – though written two hundred years earlier – might almost have been his answer to Robert Macfarlane's question: 'What do I know when I am in this place that I can know nowhere else?' For Keats, the answer was that in Cumbria he knew something about poetry, and about the living value of the natural environment, that he had never known before. Nature, he saw, had 'a countenance or intellectual tone': it was conscious; it looked back at him. It was, perhaps, a moment of shamanic initiation, which would change him.

As this anthology shows, Keats's perception has been shared by many other poets. Wordsworth (a native Cumbrian) and Coleridge (a Devon-born 'offcomer') would have agreed, as would Norman Nicholson, lifelong inhabitant of industrial Millom on the south Cumbrian coast, and the region's finest twentieth-century poet. Whether it's the magical light (something, perhaps, to do with sunlight reflecting off the sea onto the everchanging clouds gathered by an intricate mountain system), or the intense greens of the valley bottoms and the fellsides with their glittering waterfalls, or the thoughtful, articulate independence of the people who live there; there's something special, unsettling and magnificent about Cumbria which continually challenges and inspires–something that brings out the best in poets. Yet it's now more than a quarter-century since the last anthology of then-contemporary Cumbrian poets (Williams Scammell's *The New Lake Poets*, 1991) appeared.

It's time for someone to gather a new harvest, and *This Place I Know* brings home a fine body of work; its poets ranging from the well-established to relative newcomers.

Appropriately, there's a huge range in the viewpoints and subjects of these poems. Loving evocation of landscape is here, for example in Neil Curry's 'Knowing Your Place', Andrew Forster's 'Hutton Roof Crags' and Duncan Darbishire's 'Sand'. As we should expect, there's also close observation of wildlife (see, for example, Angela Locke's 'Greylag Geese Over the Solway'). And there are glimpses of transcendence: for Simon Armitage, Codale Tarn above Easedale is both a 'liquid skylight on the cathedral roof' and a kind of chalice. The finely-shaped stanzas of Kerry Darbishire's astonishing 'A Winter's Night' show the poet turned to witch or shape-shifter, 'The moon a scythe upon [her] back', soaring up until her cattle seem 'shrunk to mice and rats' as she flies above the snow. And, reflecting with a blend of historical imagination and poetic intuition, Carola Luther evokes the profound physical and spiritual kinship – both earthy and sacred – between church and byre ('St Oswald's Church, Grasmere').

But the poets are not blind to the problems of real places. Katie Hale's 'Offcomer' is tinged with smoke from the 2001 foot-and-mouth crisis; Matt Sowerby's 'Boundary' and Harriet Fraser's 'Gaps in the Duddon Valley' both confront the sadness of family farms which no one will inherit; while Cathy Whittaker's 'My Father's Desk' poignantly summons a parent beset by a related problem, the upland smallholding that can't be made to pay. Juliet Fossey's 'Sirens', full of tactile vividness – you can almost feel those bulbs – uses snowdrops to evoke the sadness of Cumbrian houses and gardens neglected whilst well-heeled owners spend their winters somewhere warm. Nor is the cold always physical: Jacob Polley's 'The Snow Prince' is a devastating poem, spoken, though not without hope, from the depths of an emotional deep-freeze.

Naturally, Cumbria's industrial heritage features vividly. Alison Barr's 'Screen Lass' makes her mark with her initials on a rock, after shifts picking out stone from a conveyor belt of coal at the pit near Whitehaven; Kim Moore's 'Walney Channel' glimpses the ghosts of long-ago workers at the Barrow shipyards, crossing a tidal path that's now almost forgotten.

Jo Stoney's 'Spirit level' has a splendidly solid and tactile account of her mechanically-skilled father and the oak-and-brass device which seems to be in her hand, steadying her touch, even as she writes the poem. Kathleen Jones, novelist and biographer as well as poet, illuminates the toughness of Cumbrian women's lives in two contrasted poems, industrial and rural: in 'Broken Biscuits' the deprivation is emotional, in 'Ginny', educational (the girl's school prize put 'on the fire' by her father).

Refracting such diverse subjects, the poems chosen here take many forms, as if each has crystallised appropriately around its voice and viewpoint. Tom Pickard (long known as an important poet associated with the North-East, but living for the past few years in Maryport) offers in the beautiful 'Winter Migrants' a poem whose stanzas resemble a series of haikus, delicate as bird-prints on a shore, yet also, to the attentive ear, carrying Anglo-Saxon alliterative sound-patterns. By contrast, Matt Sowerby's 'Boundary' uses the prose-poem form, as if snatched from a mental stream-of-consciousness. Josephine Dickinson's 'snow' presents at first sight a blinding field of type, within which one starts to make out individual words and even themes; a tract where one can dip in and out or plod forcibly ahead, dazed by the oncoming blizzard of words and sounds. Maggie Norton's 'Sea Change' shapes its stanzas as if imitating the 'sly serpent' which is the river it describes. Gillian Frances's 'Keswick Museum' is a sonnet – the perfect form, tightly packed almost to overflowing with the extraordinary collection of miscellaneous treasures which, like the Museum itself, it manages to hold.

This anthology too is a treasure-box. And now nothing remains, but to invite the reader to dip in, confident that Cumbrian poetry is flourishing into the twenty-first century and that, like Keats, many of us, both as writers and readers, continue to 'learn poetry here'.

Grevel Lindop.
July 2018

Grevel Lindop's *Literary Guide to the Lake District* won the Lakeland Book of the Year award and is now in its third edition. Carcanet publish seven collections of his poems (most recently *Luna Park*). He lives in Manchester but often walks, writes and teaches in Cumbria.

EDITORS' NOTE

This Place I Know, A New Anthology of Cumbrian Poetry brings together a collection of voices in recognition of the great and continuing tradition of Lake District poetry.

The poetry scene in Cumbria is one of the liveliest anywhere, despite the miles that separate north from south, east from west and the geographical diversity of its landscape. The wide variety of poetry groups and organisations in the county which support and develop Cumbrian talent - from Barrow Writers in the south of the county to Mungrisdale Writers in the north - is testimony to poetry's popularity. In addition to Borderlines Book Festival in Carlisle, Maryport Lit Festival on the west coast and Dalton Lit Festival in the south, we now have Kendal Poetry Festival, a new festival in the county dedicated to poetry. There are events all around the county where poetry is regularly performed, not least at the Wordsworth Trust where a past tradition of exciting and innovative Poets in Residence has kept the poetic tradition so much alive. We are delighted that poets who have spent time there have submitted poems for this anthology.

We hope you agree this vibrant collection of new Cumbrian poetry on diverse subjects and themes, captures and awakens the spirit of Cumbria in a way that only poetry can do.

Liz Nuttall, Kim Moore, Kerry Darbishire.

Kerry Darbishire and Kim Moore are prize-winning Cumbrian poets. They can be heard regularly reading their poems at events around the county and beyond. Liz Nuttall has run Handstand Press since 2005. She owned the Tinners' Rabbit Bookshop in Ulverston for 10 years.

. . .

The editors would like to say a special thank you to the following:
Jasmine Allen, who first suggested Handstand Press should publish a new poetry anthology; Rachel Ormerod, for organising and collating the submitted poems so efficiently; Ruby Evans, for her invaluable help during her week's work experience with Handstand Press; Russell Holden from Pixel Tweaks and Simon Hodson from Latitude Press, for their guidance and professional expertise; Liz Sutcliffe and Betty Towler, for much appreciated proof reading.

CONTENTS

Offcomer

Katie Hale

I come from a land that was nobody's land
and anybody's. I come from a war
of accents and blood, from heather
taking root in the bones of clans,
while the wind whispers
the old names. I come from a land
where villages are crumbled and sunk, where stories
disturb the bottoms of lakes.
I come from a land of drownings.
I come from a land where water
is ammunition hurled from the sky. My childhood
was a scrap yard of animals,
of death and disinfectant, of 4x4s and smoke.
I come from a land where rivers
unburden themselves
into farms and villages, where they carpet the city
in a rainbow of diesel and mud.
I come from the fire and the flood.
I come from a land of scythed vowels, of consonants
let tumble like ghylls down the backs of throats. I come
from a land of poems trudged across the fells
like coffins. I come from a naked land, a land
veined in stone, baring itself to the wind. My land
is bracken and gorse and the slow
gorging of ticks. My land
is height and electric skies, is water
locked behind dams.
I cannot hold my land; it is a voice thrown
back across the valley. It speaks
with the deep-throated roar of fighter planes.

No, I am not of this land. My skin is a prairie,
my hair and eyes an Irish peat and sky,
my bones a midlands town.

But put your ear to my breast.
Between my stereo heartbeats, you will hear
water, the raucous gathering of clouds.

Almost to the Top of the Hay. 10.4.14   *Felicity Crowley*

Around, the horizons are filled,
hills,fields,Cockermouth, Redmain.
I usually hear sheep
always the wind.

Sometimes the sun casts lines,
light catches the gorse
and flashes off far windows.

I always stop by the leaning hawthorn
blown over by the years
and the slate gate post.

It was here I took photos
when you were away.
How things changed,

sometimes sheep or rain,
bare branches then leaf

and stayed so much the same.

Standing on a hill

Ruby Evans

To feel the weight of the air
inside your lungs, and

see the lights of the town,
the pub you just left,

the blue darkness around you
filled with creatures

whose laws are unconscious
and unwritten, and

in the other direction,
the openness of the night sky

as if the weight of the stars
could pull you towards them.

Untitled   *Simon Armitage*

from New Cemetery

Fat brown trout (are they?)
        hammocked in amber water
                next to St Oswald's church.

That couple at Allan Bank,
        their leashed ridgeback
                slinking like a lioness.

Two kilowatt-hours
        climbing the chain-gang path,
                fighting the quicksilver spill

of Churn Milk Force
        cum Sour Milk Gill
                after a night's rain.

And for what? A true fix
        on that turtle-backed stone
                in Easedale Tarn? Not

enough. Push on
        up the wall of death,
                old boots

aquaplaning on mossed slate,
        to pond-skate
                over the liquid skylight

on the cathedral roof, to sup
        from Codale,
                from the higher cup.

St Oswald's Church, Grasmere.   *Carola Luther*

Layers. *Priors* and *befores* in the walls, storage of prayer, but also something earlier,
shifting strata of human, crow, auroch-cow - patience like the first act of building, sweat
and wattle, ivy-sap plaited by builder into pilings and branch-beams, the new-cut laths.

Shelter for all. Pebble. Fur. Straw. Curraghs of mud stuffed in and scraped. Dung
sorrel-sweet, stuffed in and scraped, slate-scraped, smoothed to a finish. Polish
of ordure and rubbing along. Shepherd, stock-stealer, nomad, farmer. Later the mystics

though the heart of this church is a byre. Functional, it has the herder's temporary
architecture, wide as a house for wintering beasts and tenders of beasts. Pasture,
valley, lake. Afterthought - a good place. Burgeoned with faith and the habit of gathering,

built-on to, built-up on, consecrated by a saint, it crumbles and remains permanent.
And under the sacrament, under services, tours, meditations of historians and Sunday
church-goers, under each flagstone walked shiny by feet, *thud, shift, faraway lowing,*

close-up pelt-press, stink-fleece, animal-heat, the walls of a stable, a Mercian fold.
Always going on, this bringing in. And there half-hidden in the rushes of the stalls,
a woman and a man. Imagine. She's thin. He has dirt smeared on his cheek. Daub

has spattered their garments, stained palms, hands to the wrists, the soles and tops
of their feet. In her brown arms, she holds a child. Exhausted, peaceful as trees, man
and woman sleep. The child opens its eyes. Stares into our eyes. Amused. Awake.

A Quaker Graveyard with Peacocks

Neil Curry

It's on the right, no more than a yard or so
before High Sunbrick Farm as you come up
over Birkrigg from Ulverston. In truth though,
when you get there, there isn't anything to see:
just another scrubby little paddock
behind a drystone wall, a bed of nettles,
a few thistles. But a plaque by the gate
says that this was once a Quaker Burial Ground
and Margaret Fox (née Fell) was buried here.

But that's all. There never was a headstone
to show exactly where. For the Friends, the body
being at best but a dark lantern
to the inner light of the soul, to draw
attention to it would have seemed like vanity,
and that, they knew, was only one step short
of wantonness. And now I think of it,
I told a wanton lie myself when I said
there wasn't anything to see up here.

What's sure to stop you stone dead in your tracks
is the Parkers' whim of keeping peacocks
on their farm. Flaunting those plumed tiaras
on their heads, they must be the swaggering
antithesis of everything that Sunbrick
and the Man in Leather Breeches entertained
when they spread their tails, flutter
the lustrous iridescence of those eyes,
and dance their stately slow pavan.

It's doubtful whether Margaret ever danced,
but it's to be hoped she saw the way the light
catches Bardsea steeplehouse as the dark
rain clouds come bruising their underbellies
over Ingleborough; and the changing
patterns of their shadows on the wet sands;
and those autumn evenings when the sunset
the far side of the bay looks like slices
of peaches. It is to be hoped she did.

The Old Chancel, Ireby

Helen Farish

Once inside, we place our hands
in the piscina, we find where the host
was stored, we read about the glory days
of the Chancel now stranded mid-field.

There are jars of wild flowers in need
of water, but when the door blows open
it isn't rain which the wind brings,
only a reminder that the weather is lord.

It would not surprise, when at last we leave,
to find horses saddled, waiting,
and rivers graced with fords –
for we are more mortal, on the *qui vive*.

unable to see the Sheila Fell landscapes.   *Alan John Stubbs*

Air dances the wings of Cherry leaves
so that green shakes about the white frowsy hair pinked in the midst
of upraised arms shaking like a child's upbraided for walking
out onto a busy street
though it is restrained by an iron cage fitted about it and into the
concrete
paving slabs diminishing what might be subtle yearnings

She has a patch, rather a coarse plaster, at her throat where
a piercing with a kind of stone is set in the wound

painfully healing. Her hair
that was wound up in a soft grey woollen towel is let down
so that what were flowers split apart and spill
about the slender bole out to the border-edges of the paving

where wall break stones tumble the corner of my eye
caught by the sleek grey of a wild cat turning away

The earth of Cumberland is my earth... *Kerry Darbishire.*

in memory of Winifred Nicholson

In the gallery vases spill windflowers, aconites,
cranesbill, lily of the valley – colours of summer
autumn and fresh snowfall reunite
   like old friends.

Dry-stone walls hold back Mallerstang Moors,
a sycamore cools the dip in a bold field as if
it's the last graze on earth. And I'm breathing fell,
   sky, sea, home – all this that lived in her

in her words,   *my paint brush always
   gives a tremor of pleasure when I let it paint a flower
   especially wild Cumbrian flowers.*

She knew the rush of light and dark,
heartbeat of blue, Payne's grey and violet –
violet she carried home from India to Bankshead –
   kept it for sunlight to dress distance in mystery

until mountains and the River Eden swept her brush dry.
I think of her pine palette – pigment leaching
like water from flagged floors on the hottest days,
   deep limed walls seeping pink,

her love of flowers in bud – promises to come
not yet arrived, altared in windows *turning air into perfume,*
how years later
   it fills this room.

Hardknott

Ina Anderson

If I had known the saints would be on my side,
that the distant sands would shift and give their salt,
that the chanting would part the clouds,

if I had known the sparrow was disguised
as a falcon, its bloodshot eyes keeping
lookout among the thorns,

if I had seen the thick sheep grazing damp-eyed
among the nettles, reaching for the celandines,
ignoring the trampled flags, the winged medals,

I might have thought to shelter by the slag banks,
to camouflage myself as a broken reed, to wait out
the long rolling glow until morning.

The wagons might have passed me by,
the dogs might have missed
the stench of last week's meat.

How might it have been if I had reached you?
If you had seen the story on my face,
the wounds, the brokenness?

How might it have been
had the pass been open, had the hawthorn
let its fruits to the ground?

Lord Warden of the Northern Marches   *Mark Carson*

…but he pestered his colleagues in London for instructions and
money so frequently, that they must have been relieved when he
resigned… (DNB)

Henry Grey on Circuit round the North,
official business, some disorder management,
sent to apply doctrinal pressure where it hurts,
to breathe in Bishop Hooper's radical ear
and bring him into line with policy,
when all at once it just became too much
and he resigned to attend to his estates.

He had estates, 'tis true, his Bonneville connection
brought him northern lands, and titles;
he might have come to Gleaston, Aldingham,
even to this bastle house on the shore;
not comfortable, certainly, the stairs exposed
on the southern wall, the ground-floor cobbled;
full of sheep at night; it stank.

But saltmarsh wrapped around, eider
and curlew serenaded; it was so quiet
even the Scots had skirted it.
Interesting times, indeed,
the young King Edward sickly,
and a bigot, and his sister lurking.
Henry's plans, such as they were,
were perilous, his daughter past thirteen,
her marriage scoped, her future doomed.

Bad company meshed him in its net;
bad talk in the smoky solar by the rocks;
and raw ambition did the rest.
He lost his head on Tower Hill.
These walls still mutter
through the soft sea-salted mortar,
the rubble buttresses and bog-oak lintels.

Humphrey Head
Chris Kelly

They say the last wolf in England
was cornered here.
After a while, you don't smell the sea
so as he ran south, keeping low,
he wouldn't have sensed the land narrowing
the limestone finger pointing
its rocky nail dropping
straight into the sea.

If he got that far,
jumping the scummy ochreous pools,
scraping barnacles with his strong and desperate claws,
there would have been no escape.
The silt would have pulled him down.
He would have drowned in the channels.

No, I see him stop
on the knuckle where the trig point stands
or just beyond
where springy turf pads the limestone bones.
He's a silhouette.
Cloud curtains trail across Arnside Knott,
the Bay shines in parallel lines behind him.
He might not have seen the dogs
but he must have heard them
howling up the wooded slope.

He turns and snarls; blue lips pulled wide,
ears flat as wind-crippled hawthorn.
His coat gapes – a white V shows
near the skin of his neck.
He backs into a question mark.
An arrow finds him - then the dogs.

Shore

Alison Carter

Old with worms, loosened by the piston

Of the lug's head, worried by gills,

tubes of blood, I disguise my infirmity

with dimples. fish scales and chevrons.

I wait for the fishermen. They are kind.

They come like midwives, dilate me

with cataracts of salt till I birth clams.

They come like surgeons, open piped

tumours, expose my black anatomy.

They explain their work as they go –

the careful forkful, the healing backfill,

how this will purge me, how I will hear

again my clean, ancient voice of shell

and skeleton drumming in a heart of ice.

White horses

Graham Austin

Today the white horses are gathering
on the pastures at Greenodd.
Since daybreak they have romped joyfully,
tumbled and jostled past us, herd upon herd.

Over Ulverston Sands, leaping and plunging,
they will go, through the Channel, line after line,
steady, determined, unstoppable.

Over Wadhead Scar and the Mussel Bed
at even pace, and still they go, split by
Chapel Island yet undeterred.

Past *The Bay Horse*, they'll stream indifferent;
then, over Plumpton Bight, swerve under
the Leven Viaduct, and struggle round Ashes Point.

The souls of drowned mariners* call encouragement
for this final push. Soon the journey is finished;
it will be time to rest. This is the way
it is till the next time they assemble.

* An old belief that seagulls are the souls of drowned sailors.

Walney Channel

Kim Moore

There's a door frame in the channel
made of thin black twisted wood.

When the tide is in, it leads to water.
When the tide is out, it leads to mud

and the beginning of the old road
across the channel. Listen at dusk

for the shouts of those who walked
that channel years ago. This was just

a crossing, the only way, before the bridge
was built. Each morning you'll hear

the shipyard siren calling men to work.
Wait and watch the path appear

like the spine of some forgotten animal
turning in its sleep before you come

to find me. Wear boots or go barefoot.
Don't stop, and if you hear them

calling, don't turn around. You'll see
barnacles and seaweed on my causeway

and a blue boat waiting at the shore.

"I open the door to my east chamber,
I sit on my couch in the west room,
I take off my wartime gown
And put on my old-time clothes."

"The Song of Mu-lan" – Anonymous Chinese Ballad (5th or 6th century)

Two hares zigzag somewhere
between dun and silver
and great arms of turbines
circle slowly on fells;

Windscale drips its poisons
where currents sweep northwards;
underground explosions
unsteady the earth;

in ministry basements
they calculate danger –
two hares zigzag somewhere
between straight line and circle –

they dress themselves carefully
in silk ties and panties;
they double the bonus,
patrol all the flashpoints,

issue statements to reporters,
spray themselves with musk.
Mulan dressed in overalls
does service as a cockler;

a hare zigzags somewhere,
its sex is not important.
She writes him a letter: *Papa,*
the work is hard, but healthy,

please don't worry,
I have wired your bank the dollars…
And sings the old ballad,
twisting the words:

my wartime gown for always,
my old-time clothes for never,
two hares side by side
slipping through borders…

5th February 2004

There are things you should know about Phoebe McCall

Kate Davis

she's only a child and smaller than small,
she lives in a house called Thimble Hall
and when she was born she was born with a caul
so she'll never drown – not Phoebe McCall.

She goes where she wants – she's no need of doors,
she can flatten her body as thin as a saw,
slip under the earth where the dark rivers roar,
swim through the sewers and drains of your town,
float like a seed of thistle-down,
then up from the drains, from plug-holes and taps,
sink, toilet, shower, bath,
she trickles and wriggles and creep like a spore.
And nobody notices Phoebe McCall –
she's only a child but smaller than small
with eyes as green as the wild Hellebore –
Do you know what she uses her sharp teeth for?

Wherever there's water she'll find a way in
to the heat of your flesh and the smell of your skin.
In bath-tubs she trawls, she slashes and mauls,
in fonts she bites as the minister calls
the names of the babies whose loud caterwauls
are caused by the teeth of Phoebe McCall –
font, river, puddle, bowl,
wherever there's water there's Phoebe McCall
and when she finds what she's looking for
her tiny teeth and her tiny jaws
will rip, bite, chew, gnaw,
flesh and bone, liver and gore –
Yes – Phoebe McCall is a carnivore.

Phoebe McCall, Phoebe McCall,
she's cunning and clever and smaller than small,
when she was born she was born with a caul –
don't think you can hide from the ravening child –
if she wants to, she'll get you – she's Phoebe McCall.

Note – A caul is an amniotic membrane which, in rare cases, can cover a baby's head at birth. Legend has it that anyone born with a caul will never drown.

Boundary

Matt Sowerby

this is the scree my ancestor toppled down. saddled and
reckless. these cobbles fell in his wake. my grandfather is an
artist. sees rugged cairns as jigsaw puzzles. has never placed a
stone wrong. my ancestors sectioned this land like paragraphs.
ruler lines on erratic slopes. parallel. unbending. no need for
cement. their wives brought them shortbread and tea
without sugar. my grandfather knows the waterfowl on the
beck. planted the apple tree my nana now harvests. my
grandfather is of this place. his children squint in offices.
i have never worked the farm. you cannot hear the peaks and
valleys in my speech. my grandfather doesn't blame me for it.
my grandfather drinks tea without sugar and watches
pointless and does jigsaws. the farm is to be sold. cobbles
dislodge from a drystone wall. i pray that i am not one of them.

Jackself's Hymn

Jacob Polley

who sits you down at
the crossroads in the dark
  which crossroads   well,
ask yourself where two paths
two tongues
two beams of olive wood
cross and he's there,
Mister Longfingers
with his scaly tunings
  you think you have
anything I want   you think
you have anything

  way back an angel got in
and was battering the underside
of heaven, his wings
on fire   hence the stars
      hence the choice among
bad choices
  hence the road dark at night and the
hearing voices
  how much to have your own
rise out of common time

Gaps in the Duddon Valley   *Harriet Fraser*

On the hill that summer's day, grey cloud hung low like a lid.
Under foot: wet grass, bracken and tormentil standing in for sun.
We passed Low Bridge Beck and Shepherd Gill,
walked beneath broad bog patches and Dawson Pike,
tracing the wall, the line between intake and fell.

We looked back along Duddon Valley, beyond Turner Hall
over a land of ruffled shadows, woodlands, rock and sky,
onto distant ridges, England's highest crumbs of earth,
across tracks followed by shepherds, for generations,
                    while above, two ravens, silhouettes, soared.

Michael's hands raised rocks as big as lambs, and heavier.
As stones were lifted, passed and teased into spaces
and boulders hauled from the chill flow of a beck,
gentle banter and laughter, like moss on rock, formed
                    around the edges of this elemental graft.

These walls, land's bones borrowed and stitched by man,
may stand solid for a century. But on a farm this size
there are always gaps, forced by unforgiving rains and snow.
Today two hundred stones are fetched, fitted, back in place.
                    Two gaps, three men, one rhythm.

Later, in the kitchen, cups of tea, cake, and Anthony's drawn face
as he tells us that Michael is leaving. All those years
treading this land, learning its ways, kenning the sheep.
His choice forced, no choice, no farm to take on here.
Now the valley has gap   a man gone, a rare breed.

There's that many, says Anthony,
raising four fingers of a weather-worn hand,
that many young ones in Cumbria who could take over a farm.
                    How will you find another like that?

On Being Certain

Josephine Dickinson

In the corner of the field I find it —
a blue ribbon frayed and tangled
with pine twigs in the furry fuzz
of its ends, the knot at the centre
intact and still shiny — yet,
what is that knot? I tied it
thinking it would make my decision clear —
slightly muddy from weeks
in the grass since it slipped off the ear
of a gimmer. When it came near time
for market I softly called them
on the field, one by one. Hope
was easy — my pet lamb, with only one
eye since the week she was born.
She ran forward and with her frantic
nuzzling hindered my faltering hands.
It took three attempts to make a knot.
Then I walked down the old quarry
for the others — Treasure, Love,
Paraclete, Faith (Hope's sister),
and even Charity, the stroppy mite,
let me grip her between my knees
as I bent down and got it tied.
Yes, it was easy. But by next day
all the ribbons had gone.
Early on the day of departure
I gathered the flock in the pen.
I tried to find again the six with names
from the ten gimmers born
this year. I was no longer sure. Except
for Hope, Charity and Treasure.
I let them all out. Later I gathered them in
one final time and as best I could made my choice.
Now the other ewe lambs and their brothers
are long ago gone. The ribbons
flutter in the field. That a-way
is how it is — being certain
which lambs I am keeping,
and which are going away,
and the reasons why.

Tramp's Barn
Irvine Hunt

I, John Rawlinson, who am a tramp
and sometimes called vagabond,
aware of a goodly barn in Stone Dale,
repaired here in snow to sleep this night
knowing as I do the dales men good and bad.
Of the Shaws, two brothers and a sister,
she stricken, sitting in their slate-floor kitchen,
a lamb rescued this icy hour from death
drying in the oven, for now alive till later cooking.
In this dale, too, Jonathan Brierley
of Fell Land who did sell his calf
to buy his childer food a treat
for their Christmas
but drank himself coinless with all he had.
And Ida Langstart, spinster,
who with sister Mabel, now dead,
did walk arm in arm to farms and cots
to scrub floors and lay out straight with
washing those bodies stiffened in the night.
But mostly farmer Isaac Slee, old and greedy,
who does burn away his time ready to take
with him every foot of land the day he dies,
and will be remembered a cruel man
though his tombstone will say otherwise.
All these are known,
as with the Lamberts who comely are
and good to wanderers with soup
and this their barn where I lie
a winter night thankful of two coats.
To all I say Amen and vow that nothing
will I thieve from here, not chickens,
nor cow's milk sucked from the udder,
nor any washing frozen and unwatched
for it is a goodly dale that has such a barn.

The Vegetable Catalogue

M. R. Peacocke

The young man came limping valentine pink
up the hill in his wellingtons. His hair
feathering in the wind like carrot leaves
was the rich orange of Danvers Half-Long
(old tapered variety, broadshouldered.)

He sat down pot-bound in his cracked boots. Please
I could do with some veg. Cooked veg and bread.
Butter please if there is any butter,
not marg. When he pulled off the boots, his heels
were rubbed through the socks to the scarlet core.

He said Do you do WWOOFS at all? You know,
WWOOFS. Working Weekends On Organic Farms.
I could weed if you showed me. Look, those beds
could do with a weed. He laid himself down
in the fast-maturing vigorous sun.

You'll burn, I said. You're burnt already. Don't
go to sleep. But he was stretched damp and fast
in his compost jacket, beyond waking.
So I went in, and cut bread in the green
kitchen light, and pricked out the arguments,

and carried the whole cautious load outside
to his print in the flattened buttercups.
If he had stayed - But if no one shows you,
how do you tell a vagrant stripling god
from the groundsel, bittercress, burdock kind?

Turning Left

Ross Baxter

This old muck-barrow,
Like the old man who used it, made
A friend of routine. For them
Each morning brought a work day,
Broken with familiar music, mended
With the same evensong: swish of a brush
Raking out the standings, the low complaint of cows,
Clank of iron rings sliding on the boskins,
Rustle of hay, the boat's prow slurp
Of mastication, rasp
Of a shovel in the grip, trundle
Of the barrow's one iron wheel over the concrete,
Driven up the slope from shippon to muck heap, drawn
Back down, always turning left, so that now
One rim is worn away. The old man too
Wore lop-sided; his balance failed,
He fell, fell ill, and died. The old barrow
Planks dried out and wrinkled with disuse,
Betrays its bias, wheels
Obstinately askew,
Still turning left.

The Heart-shaped Wood

Sue Kindon

As I heard tell, before the coming of the trees,
there was a farmer worked this windswept earth;
as love would have it, flames like corn sheaves blessed his hearth
when he first crossed the threshold with his bride.

They shared the shepherding and sheltered in stone folds
from sudden flurries. Fire showed their faces
in a gentle light, until an evil-wind -
starvation, as they called it - blew its worst.

The farmer's wife grew sick, he couldn't warm her limbs,
and when her pulse left him,
he blenched as she was lowered in the ground,
the churchyard, one quick stone's throw from the house

where, it had seemed, nothing could unseat them
from their fireside dreams.
When the embers died, his body wouldn't settle
in the feather bed, he couldn't let her go.

One aching night it came to him (or did she whisper
in his restless ear?) – he'd stake
a love-token, pacing its curvaceous form
in the hollow trysting place beside the beck,

and fill the outline of his grief with saplings, and a show of leaves.
And so sprang up the heart-shaped wood, or so I choose to believe.

Fellside Cottage Orchard

Brian Fereday

Heady apple blossom perfume

Woody arms offering charms

To the honey bees

From the wood they are drawn

Dark clamour

Around the hive.

Sirens

Juliet Fossey

Beauty calls out, like the box balls
that mark the front door.
I go round the back, loosen
the gate of Catherine's old house.
Inside the lining of my coat,
I have hidden a trowel.
As I'd hoped, Galanthus nivalis
cloak the garden's floor so thickly
I can smell them even in the chilly air.
I've brought freezer bags
for the raid, a swift flick
of the wrist and grape size bunches
come away. I shove them bagged
into inner pockets. Some tall ones catch
my eye and I split off a good wedge
to their nodding approval.
Catherine will like these when I visit,
eased into a plastic pot for the windowsill
of her room. Over tea and biscuits,
we will wonder at the new owner,
wintering in Spain, missing out
on the scent of snowdrops.

Neglect

Pauline Yarwood

I wanted to believe him, that the vet was on his way,

but he carried on hauling the cow across the yard,

a fat rope knotted to a good hind leg,

the broken foreleg loose and skewed,

and when she twisted her neck back towards me,

the stone whites of her eyes gross as moons,

I merely nodded, and walked on down the track,

past the withered ram rooting in frozen soil,

the grass trampled away months ago,

towards the ewe alone on her side,

her swollen rib-cage rising and falling

as the crows that had already had her eyes

jumped away, flapping like the black

silage-bag flags caught high in the trees.

Fallen Stock

Andy Hopkins

Come dusk the farm hands come
like evangelists
among the cattle
newly downed; few fallen stock

rise, shaking;
staggering bags with hips
loose;
they're poorly glued;

some have flung themselves
too deep
and rough-bedded
in nettle drifts

to calve any day soon;
in all this gallows light
I wish you movement, and ignorance of utility:
exhibit yourself in bellowed sound to the late light

(a still beast
becomes a dead one   largely noiselessly);

soon, but without hurry, a man will arrive
with chain and purpose and clipboard
and a shabby flatbed truck
unsuited to the terrain.

My Shepherd
Sarah Littlefeather Demick

hands
that speak
with rough and broken leather

hewn with scars
from rope and blade
and hoof and horn

ears like owls
that sense the purr
of zephyrs on the tarns

oaken shoulders
rendered by
the seasons yoke

old but broken heart
holding the secret
of the land

bones and sinews
rusty and torn

and sorrow
long aching sorrow
for all the beasts you could not save

My father's desk

Cathy Whittaker

hardly ever used made of oak,
stuffed with letters,
square, sturdy pigeon holes
for sticking bills in and old invitations
never replied to.
He never sat there for long
too busy looking after the Herdwick sheep
he was failing at making a living from,
a dream gone wrong.
On days when the rain didn't stop
he made angry attacks on forms
searched for cheque books
shouting we can't afford to use electricity
go out, pay for petrol.
So my mother would search for jobs
for him in the Whitehaven News,
and he'd refuse to do any of them.
Bad days when we kept away.
He wouldn't stay crumpled
in his utilitarian chair
even though it stormed outside,
he'd take his crook,
shrug into a torn anorak,
whistle the dog, stride up the intake
to count the sheep cropping the grass.
At his happiest outside alone,
debts, loans, jobs, pensions, wills,
all falling away
into the mist and rain
crossing the fells.

The Hawthorn on the Fell

Jean Sly

Bent by the wind's will,
Moulded by invisible force,
Time has curved your curious growth.
Twig and leaf stir and toss,
And yet your gnarled trunk is still.

At every season of the year
A tyrant wind contrives to thwart,
To crush your will to grow.
Black as death you stand
Beneath a skeleton of snow.

But buds burst on bent twigs,
And a garland of blossom
Showers forth defiance
Across May's glorious scene.

Gorse

M.R. Peacocke

Mars must be the god of gorse. Sinewy,
enduring, these stems, that can wrest sap
from dry banks and burn furious and clean.

There's not a month when gorse won't muster
a pinch of light, but now it's March, each hard bush
is bunched with gold, a hammered brightness,

yellow blossoms crowding among the forged
steel-blue spines of a new season.
Faultless and harsh, their windborne essence.

Nostrils aren't enough for it : gulp the perfume
through your open mouth, the bittersweet
of being alive, of still being alive.

Sessile Oak

Chris Pilling

By the first gate past
Newlands Church I've
a stake through my heart
but I'm still alive.

My inside is an open door
for any creature of the
fields. High above on the floor
of my fork, unseen by the farmer

who drove in the stake, a birch,
young and silver, ungnarled
with soft rust-brown bark,
is growing, corralled

well down in my cleft.
The lichens taking me
over are rare and unspoiled.
Do they think they're making me

pleased to possess them?
Do I want extra cover?
I must admit, no kidding,
I love the hands of a

lichenologist. And now
I'm aware of a healthy, new-hatched
rowan in the birch tree's fork.
We're three in one and quite attached.

Watchtree

Andy Hopkins

It begins with a phrase of birds

(yes, talk of the language of birds)

dispersed over gorse.

So it begins with phrases of birds over broom;

It begins with a paragraph of birds

weaving waste ground and marsh land into a parabola

of old magic, a wise and jittery body of magic.

So it begins with the convulsing paragraphs of birds.

It begins with the reading of sparrowhawks by birds

who read continuously the downward ribbon

of themselves, becoming reeds.

So it begins with the readings of birds.

So it begins with birds.

Goldfinches

Karen Lloyd

after Hieronymus Bosch

We are the thistle-eaters, gossipmongers
of teasel, weeds and sunflowers.

We come in like gaudy apparitions,
bring our clown-masks to the business

of seed, to the business of the feeders
under the clematis arch, our idiosyncratic

frazzle and spark, the way sunlight
filters through the fans of our wings.

In our dozens, we anoint the silver birch
with quarrel, chatter and chinwag.

But inside The Garden of Earthly Delights,
when you hungered we fed you blackberries

and carried your troubled soul upon our backs
when you were unfeathered, lost and wild.

Lapwings by Kirkside Wood

Antony Christie

their spun song hovers and wavers

as they roll as they dive

as they shape

with a sweep of the wings

with the brush of vane and barb

the hills and the shallows of air

as the upthrust holds them

their flight is their heart

as they dance to the falling note

the sky's breath taken and held

the untangling sun

at the ravelled edge of the morning

as they close as they part

as the cold fells shake and echo

This Land of Lakes

Jackie Huck

It's that wake of the dawn
      when a slow morning stirs
as the silver and blue turn to gold,
when the sun hauls itself up
      the back of the fells
and the deep darkling shadows unfold.

It's the white whip of winter
      that ices the tops, which claws
down the gullies and screes,
where the image is trapped
      on the bowl of a lake
along with a few million trees.

Or it could be the fury
      of gales through the gorse,
the cold hug of mist everywhere,
as it swarms through the valleys
      and over the peaks leaving
cool ghostly clouds in the air.

Or is it the flare from
      a flame-flooded sky that streams
into crevice and stone,
as invisible strands bind
      this land to your soul
and its splendour calls you back home.

Coming Home
Jonathan Humble

I wonder if, like me, the winter skies at Cunswick,
swathed in low cloud, above old scars of crag
and frozen garlands of brown bracken,
anticipate the welcome return of African visitors;

if underfoot, limestone bones ache for warmth,
dark fissured slabs buried beneath grass paths,
quietly longing for early May's trick of light,
tired bodies aloft after months of migration.

Do these hazels shiver with the birch and gorse,
recalling dog days, the fall and rise of darts feeding,
the speed of mameluke sabres cutting air curves
with absurd precision over woods in full leaf?

And below, flowing through Kendal's grey canvas,
does the Kent reflect colours of summer expectation,
thoughts of days spent bird watching with you,
on the long return alone to a Cumbrian terrace?

St Herbert's Isle, Derwentwater

David Scott

Island of the wild garlic
Island of the brooding geese
Island of the fallen oaks
Island of the birds in chorus
    of the lapping water
    of the sun on my page

Island of the mossy shore
Island of the stone pillow
Island of the spiritual friend
Island of the British trees
    of the roots above ground
    of the spider on my page
    of the manuscript heads of ducks

Island without ice cream
Island without notices
Island to kiss the ground of
Island to make decisions in
Island of the geese trumpeters
    of the beetle on the leaf mountain

    where oak trees grow out of oak trees
    where Bede is still read

    soft island, safe island,
    Island where you've not seen it on a bad day

    St Herbert pray for us
    St Cuthbert pray for us
    the author of the 'Anonymous
    Life of Cuthbert' pray for us

    Not that it was easy for them.
    It brought Herbert to the bone of endurance.

Island of the ministry of angels
Island of a lonely death
Island of a glorious resurrection.

Hartley's Boat

Jennifer Copley

Last night I saw my brother float away,
his ashes in a boat we'd made
from tissue-paper and bamboo.

He shilly-shallied a bit on the first few waves
as if he didn't want to go,
as if he wasn't keen on such black water.

In some of the rehearsals,
the boat had come back to us,
curving round in a huge arc to the shore.

We'd practised for months
using sugar then sand then gravel,
refining the shape,

adding a keel,
adjusting the pin-hole so it would sink
in five to ten minutes.

My brother's daughters
carried him down to the lake,
cradling him in turn,

placing a candle inside to light his way.
It was just dusk
when they let him go.

When the subject of our childhoods came up *Eileen Pun*

Faeryland, Grasmere

                    we were meeting the second time -
the cul-de-sac by the lake, where the boat hire served exotic teas.
Wonderful. To be alone at closing and not knowing each other well.
The sun god was staggering behind the hill, so we resisted any long,
sad speeches. Our kindly phrases took no longer than pedestrians
at a zebra crossing - waving, 'Thank you! So long!'

                    I wondered, does talking about childhood always
have to have something hard in it, the way a plum does or a nectarine?
I said, the saddest thing about Orlando was the - too much Disney.
For you, the hardest part about leaving Shaldon - the sea, at night.
Such force, you said. And by day? Checking for cirl buntings - their bright,
quick flights between coastline, field or tree. They could be happy anywhere.

Where is Shaldon? Oh, Devon… I've never been. Then you remembered
it was really your mother who loved the cirl buntings - their tiny
yellow bodies, their 'high risk' status, their overall vulnerability.
We agreed. So often people adopt another person's sensibilities,
for the privilege of closeness - to love something together. And this
was probably fine enough for undetermined love.

And maybe, a steaming pot of loose-leaf, Russian Caravan - shared
into two, half-filled, china cups was also fine. Shouldn't everything
delicate and dark be held to the mouth, at an axis (like a good kiss)?
And shouldn't good views be kept in platonic distance? It became chilly.
We hugged. It would be good, we said - good to meet again. Then we
thanked each other for the tea that we both loved equally.

That evening I thought about the things I could have mentioned
like my mother making me audition for kids' television. I thought
about how I never ask enough questions. I had a light dinner,
a mug of honey and chamomile that I filled twice. I took a long, hot
shower. It was so clarifying. I took so long that I missed your call.

Grasmere, 2006

Em Humble

In that moment we were placed
and poised too old for how we were at 8
Toes on slimed stones
made dry in June sun
Legs rolled up, made neat by our parents
Forced to taste sun cream on the edge of our lips

And your mum caught us in position
all 5 children in the lake and labelled famous
You, on the right, 6 months older
and now 20
mark my bedroom walls
and Christmases
Red cheeks made rosy from grinning and damson gin

But the girl in the photo on the white family wall
has falling hair
and she's scratched out her face from the picture

In March

Gill Nicholson

there is the prospect of migrating birds
who bring their courage and their certainty
with every urgent wing-beat – so
intent on coming home to nest.

How can it be that I should dread
to see those swallows flock at dusk,
criss-cross the tarn, swoop low
and almost touch each other
and the fresh grown meadow grass?

I recall, come April how
you'd count the cuckoo calls,
pause to listen for that echo
from away across the valley
trusting it to be a mate's reply.

Keswick

Jennifer Copley

When I look at the hills
I can hear my father naming them.
He would carry me on his shoulders
so I could see over walls and hedges.

I didn't mind the mountains
but I was afraid of the ogres who lived there.
I'd heard they could be seen
lying outside their caves, fast asleep,
their fat chins wobbling on their chests,
their bellies jiggling with children swallowed whole.

Dad's hands clasped my ankles,
my fingers grasped his forehead.
I knew I was safe by the familiar shape of his ears,
the smell of his hair.

Runner (a song)

Eileen Pun

[He] is at his most content in the fells, racing along a ridge, his loping gait eating up the miles and his mind up there in the mist and the cloud, appreciating the mountains, the sense of wild solitariness, and distancing himself from the clamour of the town and people.

Mary on her husband Joss Naylor, Fell Runner
From *Joss* by Keith Richardson and Val Corbett

Sunset bids him go.
While there is still light,
go before the evening of the mind.

So he leaves by back gate, and she
makes herself sideways
so that he can pass

the way a stranger would, no words
just hinge. That way,
there is nothing between them.

Instead there is the run, the getaway,
the ascent into sky, the aches
known or radical, the thresholds of rain.

What crackles underneath
his feet, his brain - what matters
is what hasn't been broken, then left

in someone else's way.   There is also the moon
that is out. His pace-setter, pathfinder, escort... she goes
by innumerable pet names.

Eventually, he passes her the way grief does -
too slow - nevertheless - go.
There is distance

to cover with stride and breath, and all that he has left.
All night, her round stare finds him all the same,
in every place he goes and doesn't plan to stay.

Ambitious, by that old definition,
        that monotonous wish: to continue,
                to elude all that eventually finishes.

        His lungs full of splinters as he runs -
            - over one fell, then the next one,
and the next one…
        A lone raven at sunrise -
            famished, restless, rakish,
                    circles the ridges.

overtaken by grazing sheep   *Anne Banks*

steep slope ahead
low gear engaged

plump little engine
purple faced
builds a head of steam
boiler about to blow
stops for water
every foot or so

I count the blades of grass
stumble tuft to tuft
puff and pant

I can do it, I will do it

spiders weave webs as I creep by
grazing sheep wander past
in the fast lane

false horizons tease me on
that last scrambled
zigzag to the cairn

such brief relief

as I arrive
they pack their picnics
stride on down the other side

my plaintive cries disturb the fells

astonish sheep and spiders

Coffin Path

Helen Mort

Who'd jog along the Coffin Path?
Most evenings only me,
hurrying between

the huddled trees,
boulders streaked with rain,
the bowed heads of the ferns,

on stones worn treacherous
by centuries – men shouldering
the dead from Ambleside.

Today, the dark's grown courteous:
shadows seem to step aside
to let me pass,

just like that summer afternoon
in Cambridge, when a hearse
gave way to me near Jesus Lane

and I sprinted on, noting the driver,
black-capped, glancing at his watch,
certain he'd overtake before too long.

Red

Tony Hendry

The lunch group volunteer
engages me in conversation.
He looks everywhere but at
the bunker-like concavity
on the left side of my skull.

Decompressive craniectomy
eased the cerebral swelling
and may have saved my life.
The legacy of flitting eyes
is something I can live with,

like his cutting up my steak,
his fixed grin, his slow talk
as to an infant or an idiot,
and his too-quick prompts
when aphasia defeats me.

He's not good at this stuff –
talking to stroke recoverers
or to anyone else, really –
but good on him for trying.
He asks about my "hobbies".

I tell him how, before this,
I loved the freedom of the fells,
and when I falter and shut up
he jumps in and says proudly
he's out there once a week.

Such clumsiness jolts him.
He flinches as if slapped.
A blush mottles his cheeks,
red as the rowan berries
in rewilded Ennerdale,

red as Solway sunsets seen
from bivouacs on Pillar,
red as the first aid blanket
that rescuers wrapped me in
so high above the valley.

Later, still feeling guilty,
he'll look up medical terms
and render me in poetry.
Most thoughts and words
that he ascribes to me

will be entirely wrong.
If asked to mark his lines,
if capable of holding a biro,
I'd be harsh for his own good.
Red. Red. Red. Red.

Sedbergh Market

Hamish Wilson

'Much busier than I thought,' says Kevin
beneath his hat. He's wrapped against the cold
but smiles as rain turns to sleet. He dives in
the van to restock the veg. Above, folds

of tarpaulin flap as the wind picks up -
Storm Eleanor's on her way. Jordan fills
our bag and, on a scrap of card, tots up,
fingers raw - back to work's a bitter pill -

'It must be tough,' I say. 'It's not so bad,
you get used to it.....at least it was dry
when we put the shelter up.' He seems glad
for such small mercies as darkening skies

spell gloom. Rain blows under the canvas brim.
'Thanks for the card,' he says, 'I liked the poem.'

The First Herdwick

Ross Baxter

When God said: "Let there be sheep",

High on a crag in Cumbria

A lump of slate cracked free to tup

A shawl of passing cloud, which, somewhat

Shocked, floated to the mountain top

And there gave birth to something

Woolly and wiley, mild eyed,

White faced, grey as frost in starlight

And with a most determined set of legs.

And God said: "What's yon?"

And Sheep said: "I's a Herdwick".

And God looked at all the sheep he'd made

And saw that they were good;

But he looked at the Herdwick and said:-

"Aye - them's the buggers!"

The Whitehaven Raid

Alison Carter

After the bread room, they could have hung
off the rigging, powdered like fops with flour,
watched the Navy boys, stupid with grog,
nurturing candles, tossing sulphur rags
onto the decks of the coal brigs, Thomson
and Saltham where they bloomed vague fire.

They could have joined the saboteurs - scuttled
over The Lime Quay , along the Sugar Tongue
with Jones, shadowed the desperate men
behind Tom Hurd Rock who hammered
a barbed stake into the touch holes, disabling
the cannons at the Half Moon Battery.

Or perhaps found a crevice on the Fish Quay
where she might have twitched her ears wildly
at him till they blurred in the half light, launched
her body frog-like in anticipatory vibration,
and he with a tiny bulge of pleasure in his eye,
might have ground his teeth with a soft sound.

But they chose to jump ship with Freeman,
Jones' man, who blew the whole thing, who
worried about the grammar of ignition,
who knew how things behaved when pushed,
who smelt the sweet grass of burnt tobacco,
the blue blaze of overproof rum, liquid promise

in a warehouse full of sugar and molasses.
It consumed the night air, as he ran towards
Marlborough Street to give the warning,
hearing only the scrambled syncopation
of rats claws, amplified, loud as conscience,
on the irregular setts beneath his feet.

A Woman Made Out of Paper

Judy Brown

*for Phoebe Johnson (d. 2005) who kept a scrapbook record of
Grasmere life from 1951 to 1976*

I imagine her: lamp-lit, scissors in hand,
some kind of gluepot and brush on her desk.
There are those who recall her later years,
adrift in the Abbey Home, thirsty for paper,
handling her scrapbooks to kindle the past.
As a stranger myself, I'm just dreaming her up
from these fidgety scraps, a mash of elderly
newsprint and the occasional photo, like this:
her passport (I like her brow, and her round,
emphatic black glasses). I'll prise her whole,
if I'm deft, from what's stuck to the thick tan
pages, her friable palace of reportage and paste.
There must be traces: spots where the newsprint
is still live enough to catch fire. I want
to prove that paper turned out to be stronger
than she hoped. Next I'll test each yellowed entry
for warmth – the story, say, from 1961 –
when Grasmere froze, and marsh gas, rising, flamed
at the holes two men had pierced in the ice.

Echo at Blake Rigg, Pike of Blisco   *Deborah Hobbs*

I stand on the stone and shout,
like an argument in an empty room.

Big voice, boom box of the mountain,
do you hear the real me?

Do you hear the tragedies of the sea?
They are dumping them like old huts.

They are dumping them like old maps.
Are we the refuse of the earth?

I test your magnificence, utterance,
codes of bouncing back,

a single reflection of love,
love, love…

We are a chamber of love,
that renders love a stone.

Castle Crag, Borrowdale   *Deborah Hobbs*

Millican Dalton born in Nenthead, Alston, Cumbria (1867-1947) self-styled 'Professor of Adventure,' lived as a guide and hermit in a cave dubbed 'The cave hotel'

The man you swore you once saw, I never saw -
too young to step between rocks and spy the entrance
like a giant's mouth dripping with algae and slime -
he was the man who blagged a tip each time
he showed remains or someone else's place
over the residue of a cliff. He was more image
than passion, more passion than image;
an awkward humility like a seed struck on him.

Day and night watched his words spread;
bright as a glossed voice catching on the wind,
bright as a wishbone in a riddle of stones.

What could he tell of wisdom from where he stood;
the crag unashamed in fern and close, sandstone
and tuff? His body like a broken wheel one year
when the tail end of a storm strung his lungs like memory;
a verdant homespun miraculous hue of light and air
spinning walls like a bat, like a travelled thing.

Long Meg and Her Daughters   *Geoffrey Holloway*

I've skimmed what bumph there is, of course:
stuff about barrow markers, Druidic worship,
a witch's curse turning red stones to blood.
One thing's for sure though: this is no accident,
no outcropped quirk, neolithic folly.
Something's about here that rounds off an era.
Long Meg for instance, what's she?
The ghost of a sarcophagus somewhere else?
A bumptious, home-compelling lingam?
A prod of belly with matriarchal slit beneath?
And the entourage, what's that? A clan? A coven?

Speculating, I go walkabout.
A sentinel ash glints in the wind,
its leaves a shoal of minnows.
A jet goes over, a snarling pipefish.
The smell of cowpats, glistening wheel hubs
mobbed by ginger dungflies, comes up strong
-after this surely the nose stays sceptical?
I look at webs trembling in sandstone pocks,
at grass happened in cracks, spiral patterns,
the scratched initials of some stray tourist,
at this, that. Suddenly find myself stood
in the middle of it all, my head a Bronze Age whirlpool;
still awed, by what doesn't matter.

Sunkenkirk Stone Circle *Caroline Gilfillan*

Below the trouser cuffs of Swinside Fell
Sunkenkirk opens its midwinter mouth
to our muddy boots. Stone elders watch
as we run fingers over the blips and dips
of porphorytic slate, tracing rain's worry lines
between moss and lime-bright lichen.

It's rumoured the devil pulled down walls,
chucked bricks in the mud night after night
when men tried to build a church here.
The stones looked on, laughing at the idea
that the messy world and its teeming creatures
could be contained within four walls and one book.

The sheep watch, unperturbed, as we examine
the fifty-five stones – the tall and the fallen.
Walking back to the car down the rocky track
we talk of the hush of the circle, its long
endurance in this wind-sighed valley,
how sunlight fills the bowl of the bay below.

Screen Lass

I
She hurries up to High Kells,
white skirts billowing.

Saltom cliffs are a red drape,
hemmed with dark seaweed,
tugged by the tide.

The horizon as thin
as a tern's wing.

She climbs down into shadows
of sea-salt and sandstone
and begins to carve.

Her initials curve
in loops of bird flight,

next to a fossil
locked in stone.

II
Now bent to her job,
she picks out slate and stone
from the coal.

After the long shift at Haig Pit
she flies along the coastal path,

runs her finger
around the smooth grooves
of her name;

bright, red, eternal.

Maryport Coastal Path, late October 2016 *Kelly Davis*

(Between the Brexit referendum and the US election)

In this wind-scoured place,
at the back end of the year,
water, earth and air combine
and lay themselves down,
exhausted, supine.

The itchy grass peels away,
down to the scabby shingle,
and further down,
to the ribbed sand,
and further still – to the sea's plasma shimmer.

The land wrenches itself out of fertility.
A few clover blossoms cling to flimsy stalks
in their dusty pink cardigans,
deaf to the whispers
of their dry brown sisters.

The bramble bushes have lost their jet earrings.
Their tattered leaves are the colour of dried blood.
A red builder's crane rears up like a harbinger.
The boat masts – brittle as twigs –
catch at my heart.

The next time it rains

Clare Proctor

The next time it rains the children are afraid.
Rain had proved a hard master,
had beaten them with angry fists.

Before, when water had touched them
it had been tender; had slipped from their skin,
risen up their legs as they eased
into the river; sprinkle-kissed them
as they watched the washing
of the horses.

Water had been a villain elsewhere,
had dressed up on the news, appeared
in distant countries, where the toll of death
dripped from BBC lips.

But now, when rain drums
on the asphalt roof, eyes
grasp each other
like drowning men.

Mellbreak

Tony Hendry

Crow-black country nights.
Headlights sweeping narrow roads.
Callow drivers cornering too fast.
Unbelted passengers swaying, sliding.
Arms out of windows, palms tom-tomming
on rust-flecked Ford Cortina doors.

Many years ago this was,
before laminated Prove It cards,
when bar staff in Cumberland wilds
were more tolerant than those in town.
Friday nights, carloads of sixth formers
drove to the Kirkstile Inn and back

and, by a miracle, none died.
None were more alive than then,
when risk and beer slew devils.
Essays and swotting could wait.
Our respite, doing as we pleased,
like climbing Mellbreak at closing time.

Was it a bet or a dare? I forget.
Seven of us took up the challenge,
going *diretissima* by moonlight,
scaling the steep ridge behind the pub,
watched by scornful Herdwick sheep
and the silver eyes of two lakes –

Crummock Water, Loweswater.
Halfway up, I fell and gashed my wrist,
and the blood looked like black ink
by the moon. Two hankies staunched it –
mine tied to the one Lynn offered –
then onward to the summit cairn

which Luke reached first. Of course.
Hill farmer's son used to herding sheep,
county-standard runner, our top bloke.
High fives were yet to be invented,
so we all shook hands, jigged around
and howled in triumph at the moon.

My wrist still shows the scar.
Sometimes, on this sublunar path,
I track white bridge over blue vein
and recall swift, sure-footed Luke
back then on that Mellbreak climb.
First among us.... to run out of time.

Wet.

Solomon Russell-Cohen

(At Devil's Bridge.)

People jump off of Devil's Bridge, toes curled
around the edges liked they'd promised in maths,
worried about their shorts coming off.

I go swimming there, normally on grey
afternoons with Hannah, when
it's not busy, there's less people with nicer
bodies. Hannah shouts at them - the lads

lined up like stupid skinny milk bottles - she
storms over mid-sentence,
like shooing away pigeons from her food,
yells from the bottom;

points to the memorial facing
the wrong way, and widens her gaze.

I never say anything. I should - but they jump in,
don't die, keep their promises
and their shorts on - I don't have to feel bad,
as they float down the river like twigs

Sand

Duncan Darbishire

And I was young and waist deep in the River Kent,
halfway between the Arnside shore and Humphrey Head.
The tide was at its lowest, dragged out to the far sea,
gathering its power, ready for the inward rush,

its bore roaring through the rills, sliding over shoals,
faster than a man can run, scouring sand and scar.
Here level land is laced with sweeps of mercury,
its shallow gullies carved by moon-pulled pendulums

of liquid light - flood tides that pervade a desert,
wide and wet, where voices come, not go, no one lives,
where winter waders pipe aboard the wanderer
who wades the shimmery haze, walks out west from Hest Bank

through blind quicksands, the quags of watery granules
that wait the unwary. Where sand and sky collide
long lines of stunted brogs implanted by the guide
designate a safe route through this land rendered fluid
beneath the ebb and flow of the changeless changing sea.
And I was young and new and walking Morecambe Bay.

Greylags over the Solway : After Bird Flu *Angela Locke*

Beyond the great barn which rears red over my land,
A thumbprint of dark swirls above a rainbow,
Reveals itself fluid, a comet presaging change.
Blind eyelets of doors turn to catch the sound,
The wild sobbing cry of returning, joy,
As greylags run ragged over the fell edge,
Mocking the shadow of Criffel's watery sketch.
And they are coming down, so tired they forget formation,
Following the curlew call I heard at milking yesterday;
The scream of lapwings.

I know they will have my Spring wheat,
Crap in my yard, disturb lambing ewes in intake fields.
I know it, yet I love this coming down of geese
Into my high field, low-winged as they skid the ditch,
The dry stone walls, this flop and strut as though there was
Nothing to it after all, this long journey between continents.
Now they tell us I must fear them. Perhaps they bring death;
I must look for corpses, pen my ducks, keep the free range hens inside.
My sheep stand clumped against the invasion,
Their field tagged with droppings, their heaf.

We've all worked hard, this long winter
Above the Solway where the rain stacks like a black shook.
Lambs, new-born, wet-slicked with love and afterbirth
Are vulnerable against this wind, this wet.
I've seen too many deaths.
I need this blessing of geese; this benediction.

A Winter's Night

Kerry Darbishire

after The Song of Wandering Aengus – W.B Yeats

Geese safe inside, I shut the door
and turned into the frosty night,
left settling chatter, rustling straw
four still white wings tucked warm and tight.

The Plough above the sycamore
and Seven Sisters clear to see,
the green and red lights in the north
like sailors' lanterns on the sea.

Then in a breeze I lifted through
November branches high and bare,
bones needle-thin and shining new
my feathers glided brimmed with air.

The moon a scythe upon my back
and frozen scent of earth below,
my cattle shrunk to mice and rats
as I flew silently as snow.

Though now it seems I'm almost blind
to trodden pathways long ago,
in hope I'll search until I find
tracks in a land I used to know.

Lazarus

Geoffrey Holloway

Two things about the old byre:
a broken window
and a martin's nest.
One the work of boys no doubt:
chucking stones from a mark
till no glass tinkled,
they could lounge off,
random feathers in the hair;
the other, art of a parent bird –
forked lightning whisper-shafting through
till dusk found its diving tail
in a pocket of drowsy mouths.
And was there a third thing?
Maybe a touch of myth:
the blind eye opened
on avid,certain grace.

snowsnawesnauwsnausnauesnasnaasnousnovsnowesknowesnosnoosnouhsnowhsnawsno
wesmoltesnowssnowinharvestsnowinsummersnowonthemountainsnowwhitesnowbanksn
owbedsnowbergsnowblastsnowblocksnowbridgesnowcavesnowcloudsnowcoversnowcru
stsnowflurrysnowglaresnowhutsnowlightsnowpatchsnowsquallsnowicesnowlinesnowlan
dsnowboundsnowmistsnowmountainsnowoozesnowpeakssnowplainsnowrackssnowridge
snowriversnowrucksnowshintesnowshowersnowslidesnowslipssnowslopessnowslushsno
wsquallssnowshipssnowstatuessnowstreamssnowboatssnowsunshinesnowswellssnowtrac
kssnowwindssnowanchorsnowboardsnowbootsnowbuggysnowchainsnowcoatsnowfences
nowgallerysnowgaugesnowglassessnowpantssnowscoopsnowscootersnowshedsnowspect
aclessnowstakesnowsuitsnowtractorsnowtyressnowvehiclesnowshoesnowskatesnowback
edsnowbeatensnowblanchedsnowblownsnowbornsnowboundsnowchokedsnowcooledsno
wdazedsnowdimmedsnowdrownedsnowfedsnowhoodedsnowpackedsnowdazzledsnowsh
oulderedsnowbeardedsnowblanketedsnowboweredsnowcappedsnowcrestedsnowsuitedsn
owrubsnowswathesnowsnowhungsnowcrownsnowdriftedsnowdrivensnowdrownedsnow
encircledsnowfeatherdsnowhairedsnowhoodedsnowimpededsnowladensnowlimbedsnowl
inedsnowloadedsnowmantledsnowsnowrobedsnowrubbingsnowscarredsnowsuitedsnowti
ppedsnowtopdsnowtoptsnowtoppedsnowwhitenedsnowwingedsnowwroughtsnowcasting
snowclearingsnowdroppingsnowblowersnowbreakersnowclearersnowgatherersnowloader
snowmeltersnowscrapersnowshifterssnowthrowersnowsnowbrightsnowbrilliantsnowclears
nowsnowdeepsnowfairsnowproofsnowsoftsnowbeltsnowblanketsnowblinksnowblossoms
nowflakesnowbonessnowbreakssnowbuckingsnowbunnysnowconesnowcoursesnowcrafts
nowcreepsnowcripplesnowcruisersnowdevilsnowdroppersnowsnoweatersnowfiresnowfo
otsnowgrainsnowgunsnowmakersnowholesnowhousesnowjobsnowlimitsnowmachinesno
wballssnowmansnowpicksnowsnowmadsnowdrunksnowfaintsnowtiredsnowsheltersnows
nowscenesnowbrisksnowdrumsnowbellsnowloftsnowwolfsnowleopardsnowcatsnowhare
snowdogsnowhazesnowstormsnowmeltseasnowsnowdazesnowbluesnowfastsnowcoopsn
owdazzlesnowsuresnowsillsnowsocksnowseatsnowthronesnowmindsnowsnowdrips
nowgripsnowwatchsnowhatsnowgazesnowwhelmsnowgoosesnowskeinsnowsadsnowstar
vedsnowsuckedsnowpockssnowdimpssnowshearsnowgodsnowsensesnowhuesnowpanes
nowburnsnowstainsnowsnowsnowstitchsnowsnowhairsnowlocksnowcabinsnowwristsno
whengesnowstaresnowstairsnowbeadsnowfingersnoweyesnowlegsnowwaistsnowlapsno
wsnowblizzardsnowachesnowknucklesnowpucksnowkneesnowshinsnowheartsnowbreath
snowtwinsnowsnowsnowprismsnowwindowsnowwinnowsnowbreezesnowcakesnowboo
ksnowsilencesnowsnowbeastsnowgashsnowguestsnowgustsnowrainsnowbentsnowhensn
owtrancesnownecklacesnowmailsnowfollysnowtroutsnowsnowsnowmerchantsnowpacks
nowpelletsnowplanesnowqueensnowrakesnowrollersnowscapesnowsheensnowsleepsnow
snakesnowstonesnowtansnowtimesnowbearsnowcamelsnowfishsnowfleasnowflysnowgn
atsnowinsectsnowmousesnowpanthersnowsnowwormsnowcocksnowpartridgesnowpheas
antsnowflightsnowbuntingsnowfowlsnowgrousesnowhammersnowfinchsnowowlsnowyo
wlsnowsnowpetrelsnowpigeonsnowquailsnowsparrowsnowapplesnowbushsnowgemsno
wglorysnowgrasssnowgumsnowlilysnowmouldsnowpeasnowpearsnowplantsnowrosesno
wtreesnowedsnawesnausnowesnawedsnaadsnaatsneusnewsnewesnawensnawnsnowensno
wnsnewnsnowberrysnowbirdsnowbrothsnowcladsnowcoldsnowdriftsnowdropsnowfallsn
owfieldsnowsnowsnowflecksnowflowersnowishsnowlesssnowlikesnowsnowmobilesnow
ploughsnowsnowsnowwatersnowsnowwreathsnowysnawysnawiesnowiesnoweysnowears

The snow falls forever

Mark G Pennington

Woken again in the fifth hour to darkness,
and memories of a shattered voice who cannot
leave his lover, and from the pretty recent
past the Romanian honey breakfast, a train to
Windermere, the bookshop at the corner of
the station; then where all light fades as a shadow
comes home to the maisonette, a place for
the homeless, a place halfway here, halfway
there, halfway to nowhere, and the scent of a
cheap winter breeze hanging in the air, the
snow falls, and there is no post today, no schools,
no yoga, no horse racing, and the toy
companies collapse; up with the blinds
and hit by the blinding light, the earth turned
to white, the earth with all its worms, then
back to bed where the heat tenderly gathers
beneath the coverlet, and awoken again by shouts,
go to the window where a fight breaks out,
the taller one with the bobble hat and the
smaller one tussle it out in the snow, swinging
each other like blushing roses in a burning
wind, and the taller one grabs the other guy's
rucksack and tosses it over the balustrade and
into the cold river, and it reminds me of a bird
fight I saw last spring, where one big seagull
trapped a blackbird beneath its feet and
pounded that bird until it faked its own death,
and when the seagull came back it took its
opportunity and tossed itself into the cold river;
the smaller guy came back looking for
something in the snow, he started kicking the
earth and then left.

Of Love and Mountain Tops   *Polly Atkin*

You need it to say something real, something
of love and mountain tops. Of pacing
the thin gallery of your days here, travelling
nowhere, tracing and retracing your trail,
translucent in low light. About living
step over step, unable to break
the pattern. You wanted to mean about running
away from all that, the closed circuit, the bloating
museum of your life, over-layered. The galloping
panic that you've become stagnant. That locked
outside of time you are barely alive
and can never return to it. However you put it,
the invisible structure that keeps you in stasis
is genetic, grows from you. Your being creates it.

You need it to say something about walking outwards,
into the back-pushing wind, pathless.
You wanted to speak the stars, of branches
fragmenting the sky. Of the moon and the water.
Of them acting together. Cold on your forehead.
About seeing it clear from above, flying
in dreams, or stood on your own concrete feet –
sea to the west, the moon a whole,
and the future coming to meet you, though
you can't make it out. You can't make it out.
This is the clarity that comes with hurt.
You don't know the words, or if they exist,
but you keep stumbling on, keep grasping. You must.
It sings of love, and mountain tops.

The Dogs

Helen Mort

Some mornings, waking up between the sandy whippet
and the black – their breathing slow as mine,
their eyes more sorrowful – I remind myself I'm not a dog.

It's not acceptable to taste the grass or roll in moss until
I'm musked with it. There are deer in the woods I'll never see.
My thirst discriminates. It does not have me bend

my grateful head to puddles, gutters, hollows
in the rock. I don't track rabbits in my sleep.
I'll not know love like theirs, observed in mute proximity

and if I sometimes sit bolt upright after dark, sensing
a movement in the yard, it's only that I've learned
a little of their vigilance. I'm not like them:

one night I'll set off past the meadow, down
behind the beck, beyond the blunt profile of Silver Howe
and nobody will call me back.

Judgement Day

Helen Farish

*Michelangelo requested that his body be buried in Santa Croce
so that on Judgement Day the first thing he'd see would be
Brunelleschi's cathedral dome.*

I'd be under the apple tree
not far from the daffodils
which every spring spell ANNE.

Dad cutting the grass
would be the first thing I'd see.
Don't die again, the first thing I'd say.

Somehow it became everything –
the cobblestone house, the barn,
the yard like a stage,

the ghyll view, clothes drying in winds
which had names, and the sycamores
I called Father, Son and Holy Ghost.

And each day we laid innocently
on top of the last dug our names deeper.
Spring will always bring them back

in the distance between the Keswick apple
and the back door, the slight incline,
the lilac, the old swing swinging

as though I'd just jumped off,
aged ten, my whole life
behind me.

The Snow Prince

Jacob Polley

My mother was a distance, blue with ice.
My father too, demonstrative as snow,
drifted away from me, cold in the face,
when touching might have put our love on show.

But who would we have shown, the curtains drawn,
the two of us alone in rooms where fires
ate up the dark and I, like paper torn
from his, enfolded all the old desires?

Yes, to see yourself but not to touch:
desire is old, but prohibition older;
and when they saw themselves in me, so much

deep-frozen in my parents held to the colder
customs to which they had both been exposed.
I right it here. I touch the rimed wound closed.

I used to know these things

Geraldine Green

The season for shrimps and
a sign chalked on blackboard
'shrimps second cottage on right'
the names of trees in
Bardsea woods.
I used to know them
I used to know these things.
The name of Bill Stables' dog
that trotted behind him
as he rode his bike to Baycliff
to catch the tide
the sight of Gillam
padding barefoot round
his grocery shop in town.
I used to know the feel of a
lapwing chick in my hand
taste of wild strawberries
taste of a new laid egg
my dad had found in the hedge
on his way home from his shift
at Glaxo. I used to know
the feel of wind on bare skin
when I ran through bracken
smell of mud its soursalt tang
sound of the buzzer at Vickers
sight of thousands of men pouring
out through the yard's iron gates
on foot, on bikes, in cars.
Sight of the first primrose
hidden among gorse
and always a kestrel hanging
on the wind above the clifftop
always the sound of the Irish Sea
always that taste
sweet as a nut
of freshly peeled shrimps
hauled in, loaded onto tractors, driven
over mudflats across the Bay
I used to know.

Sometimes You Think Of Bowness

Kim Moore

and swans on the pier being fed by hand
and the ice cream shop with twenty six flavours
and the wooden rowing boats like slippers

and how Windermere is one place and Bowness
another, and just a stretch of road joins them
together, of the hotel on the hill, the Belsfield

and Schneider, walking down to take the steamer,
his waiter following with breakfast on a silver tray,
but mostly you think of the people, drawn to water,

and how it looks in the rain, as if the shops
are made of water, of ducking into a doorway
and carrying the smell of rain inside.

Wild Swimmin' Women

Kelly Davis

A sisterhood of Cumbrian naiads,
you come to life in icy lakes and tarns,
risking death by hypothermia,
revelling in bone-tingling chill.

You bring us accounts of your joyful battles
with sub-zero temperatures,
dispatches from the front line
of human endurance.

I am made of weaker stuff.
But I like to think of you out there:
laughing and gasping as you take the plunge,
your rosy faces glowing like beacons.

Ulverston to Lancaster train 10.28 am *Caroline Gilfillan*

These women cram the carriage
with their open-gob cackles,
their knots of laughter rough as rope,
throwing their heads so far back
you can count their teeth. And now
they're singing along to a tiny speaker,
lifting their voices high as their skirts,
the tune sweet as fudge in their mouths:
Baby you can fuck yourself.

A pink haired girl is snogging a lad
who can't believe his luck, making
other travellers tut and grumble,
but I'm riding the roller-coaster
of whoops and yells, admiring
the sheer front of the revellers,
their lush eyelashes and glossy hair,
the way they make a racket, take up
so much room and don't give an inch.

One zips open her suitcase to extract
bottles, glasses. Fizz is poured and
handed round, its grapey perfume
kissing the smudged windows as the train
pulls out of Grange, across the marsh
and sandy ribs of the bay, past sheep
with full grown lambs. A little apart
from the shrieks a young woman
sits quiet, shy, in her tiara and veil.

In Over Through Off

Christine Cochrane

Sizergh Castle, December 2017

In the castle café on Fridays
over regular cappuccinos women knit
through life's patterns, colours. Cast
off
    with grandchildren, retirement,
        recipes, remedies, illnesses, diets –

        … In Vogue Felice a twin
        set designed especially for
        the not-so-slender

        fast-dyed exclusively
        to Marshall & Snelgrove's own
        fashion colours - Azure Cloud,
        Frost Rose, Plum Wine, Chinese Aqua,
        Panama Sand, Sage Leaf and Burnt Honey….

        … this dainty yet cosy bed
        jacket in Target Cherub
        Baby Wool flatters…

In the café clatter they knit and natter
over scones and jam. Plain and purl
through pullover patterns, sharpen needles. Cast
off
    give men a ribbing
        over sheds, slowness, solitude -

        Knitters …
        … look for this knob;
        only Aero knitting needles
        have the perfect point
        not too sharp to split
        the wool
        not too blunt
        tapering
        just right for speed.

They do not, cannot
look each other in the eye
in case they drop a stitch.

        (Found poetry in italics from 'Vogue Knitting' 1947)

Not a Nature Poem   *Ann Grant*

This is a not a nature poem, because
when I crunch through those red leaves and the squirrel dashes
from that magnificent oak into the woods at the back of Kendal Green.
I just think about how, with our elongated vowels, we say O-o-o-a-a-a-k.
When my face is frozen, even though I'm wearing my favourite hat and gloves,
I find a conker on the ground and take a photo with my i-phone
just so I can photo-text you that
'Love conkers all' joke again.
When I listen out for the sound of fireworks
because you love them so much and I notice the kids
have started to collect wood for a bonfire.
You are all I think about.
This is not a nature poem and it's not a romantic poem because
how could I describe all of this
or talk about love differently.
This is just a poem from me to you to say
"Another year babe and we've made it and we're being the best we can be"
and you know that 'Love conkers all' joke.
Well it's not really a joke.

Rannerdale bluebells   *Juliet Fossey*

They are the maps of our missing woods.
Every spring you can see them,
thousands of little blue under-lights;
luminous, lovely.

They should cast their cerulean haze
like a cloudless sky beneath chapels of trees,
wafting scent of hyacinth;
elusive, sweet.

But sheep nibble the emerging saplings,
taking alder, rowan, birch, oak.
Sharp incisors render the ancient seed bed
invisible, empty.

The bluebells still shine,
waiting for cover, a return to dappled light.
What if they went, burning out one by one?
The maps of our missing woods, gone.

Knowing your Place   *Neil Curry*

Not far along the road that crosses
Kirkby Moor, there's a stand of sycamore,
A dozen or so, their tops rounded
And buffed by the wind. Then comes the long slow
Slope of Benson's Hill on up to Horrace.

Away to the left, neglect has bewitched
A hawthorn hedge into a camel-train
Of trees climbing against the sky-line.
Horrace is a child's drawing of a house.
A right turn there takes you down to Lowick.

It's a walk I feel I have perfected.
I know the gate where the piebald ponies
Come dribbling down to have their noses rubbed;
Where brambles, as they die, take on the red
Of Indian leather, and where the Coniston Hills

Begin to unfold. One more right there
Brings you in no time to a tarn. Nut Hollow, or
Knotallow? No one seems sure.   But a place
Is its own mind, and to know it truly
Is like knowing a poem: it isn't always

What the words mean that matters, but what is heard
In the silences – in the tension that exists
Between the pulls of memory and feeling.
From now on it is the sound of running water
That will be with me all the way down

To Newbiggin; to a farmhouse sheltered
By a tight fold in the hill, and built
Out of the hill. Making no claims to a view,
It is what is meant by belonging:
A collaboration and an atonement.

The Fells Whispered Goodbye   *Hannah Hodgson*

I live around fells
who used to come home with me,
earth clinging to my boots
staying long after being washed off.

There is nothing comparable
to the invisible slap
of wind against your cheek,
not painful, exhilarating.

I remember those fells
hurt me more than others.
I looked around the cloakroom
wondering if anyone else

was screaming on the inside.
If the fells had ripped off their skin
without them falling.
In the days before diagnosis'

It's as if the hills knew
I wouldn't be back again
and so unpeeled the sky
pointed to the sun as it set.

The fell wrapped its arms
Around my shoulders,
whispered 'goodbye' in the wind
and let me go.

Kip Law before dawn, early January   *Antony Christie*

by fading stars and no moon
I have climbed to the three
dykes' meeting,
to the finger cairn
crooked eastwards
beckoning more light,
to the one flat rock,

unwrap my sandwiches
on a beach of bleached grass,
drowned flotsam knots of
broken winter heather,
where a stirring grouse
blasts me with barking
and wing blather.

mist waves lap
on a dark far blue
as the Cumbrian fells
make fins in a rippled sea –
a shift of wind,
a temporary portal,
where a green eye

stares at me bright as
new grass after the silage cut,
a finch's breast,
the curled spring holly,
blinks shut
at the hesitant touch
of a pale edged sun.

Hutton Roof Crags

Andrew Forster

This is land reduced to its bones:
a tattered map of runnels and grikes
carved by millennia of rain, stretching
beyond sight. Scrabbling on to
the limestone pavement on Holme Park Fell

the motorway behind is in clear view
but oddly silent like a waking dream.
Wind rattles through dried hawthorn and ash,
blown in, seeded in the thin soil of clefts,
twisted postures like a visible breeze.

It's hard to balance on the tilted rock
and rifts open out before us, forcing
shifts of direction. It's easy to get lost here.
This place shrugs off any meaning we impose.
Scattered erratics are signs we can't decipher.

Resting by a boulder, my fingers find
an ammonite in a crevice, in perfect relief.
We wonder at melting ice that brought it here
and strange peace that kept it undisturbed
and leave it as a gift for the next stranger.

Moving on, it's easier not to look
for a fixed path, but put faith in patterns
of limestone. Out of the corner of my eye,
a blue butterfly rises from a brittle bouquet
of hart's tongue, briefly charging the air.

Alpine

Phil Houghton

Sharp Edge will not
allow nerves a foothold.

Grasping fingers

seek a fracture,

drawing me up,

face-to-face

with this rock splitter,

the Starry Saxifrage

- white and tiny and celestial -

bobbing in the breeze

of my gasping breath

as though tethered

by a hair

to the back

of this beast.

Saxifraga stellaris on Sharp Edge, Blencathra
– rock breaker, from Latin: saxum frango

Visibility

Charlie Lambert

Is it a path,
or a beck?
Are we climbing,
or tumbling?
Cairn? Or simply stones?
Cloud? Or mist?

The compass dithers
and the trig point
lurks damply
within the mist.
Winterbrown bracken
slopes across the crag
and black marshes suck
our footsteps backwards.

Then it comes without a sound
without a movement
without a sign
or a breath.
The veil parts,
and far below,
below the bracken
and the becks,
three hundred feet below,
the lake appears,
and silver streaks illuminate
the steel grey surface,
always changing,
changing yet permanent,
seen, or unseen.

The view
Graham Austin

'There was a gate,' she said, 'we could have parked!'
We could have done; *I* could have done.
'The view is nowhere near as good from here.'

I stopped, reversed into a field, returned.
'The other way, the other way is what we want.'
It was, of course, 'the other way'; I knew.

Back the road we'd come a minute since, I
smoothly, most obligingly continued,
came athwart the crossroads, proceeded over,

stopped, reversed, retraced our route, and came to rest.
'There, isn't it?,' she said. 'A better view?'
I switched the engine off; it was a view most beautiful.

Old Mine Rescue Station

Hilary Tattershall

Today spring sun drills through
long barred windows, casting a cage
on the polished plank floor.
A brattice of sofas cosied in throws,
granny squares unless I'm mistaken,
and corners butted with cushions
support newly painted walls.
Even now memory lingers cold
while dust motes dance carefree.
I stand to the side of a proddy rug,
not wanting to dirty it with my boots,
and gaze at a framed print
on the sealed chimney breast: an impression
of heaps, a wagon and helmeted men.

The Piano in the River

Karen Lloyd

They found you in the gorge
below the bridge -
strings pebbled shut

now bluebell-hummed
the chip and chisel water
plucks your tongue

underwater weather-babble
assonant salmon-run stream
play me your variations
hear dragonflies click-sing
extemporising into flight
(exuvia diminuendo)

set to sunlight through new leaves
and over your water-thrummed strings
mayfly spin
to thrush music
to blackbird recitative

the moon's a troubadour
fragmented in the midnight stream

I'm listening still -
the ones who threw you in,
they couldn't hear you sing.

Reading Rooms

Nicola Jackson

The way the rippled smoothing
    of the horse hair plaster feels
        the surface of ancient fingers,

touches the cut iron latch
    fashioned across the lonning
        in the village forge.

The way the winter sun
    lights the soft red sandstone
        almost from within.

Curved marks cut the gable wall,
    sickles sharpened by youthful hands
        or the gunnels of the rain.

The day we entered these low rooms
    and felt a coming in
        that would never leave.

Keswick Museum

Gillian Frances

Here be curiosities. Keep your wits
about you. Look - penny farthings, suspended;
owls, fossils, muskets, a dead cat, the splendid
hornfels xylophone. A sharp-nosed fox sits
on a box; Flintoft's vast, raised, glazed map fits
neatly on a wall, its bulk upended,
its named lakes and brown mountains defended
by a rail. *Don't lean!* Stone-age axes, bits
and pieces of provincial history so
numerous they spill into this sestet,
which was reserved for the Exhibition:
a white sea broken by an archipelago
of paintings, letters, diaries - the alphabet
of memory, the stuff of re-transmission.

Wordsworth for a Local (fragment) *Chris Pilling*

He was not a man folks could crack wi',

not a man as could crack wi' folks.

You could tell fra the man's faace his potry

would niver have a laugh in it. No Wordsworth joke!

Many a time I've seed him a takin'

his family out in a string and stoppin' behind

a gaping, akin

he was to an.... (here he couldn't find

The word he was after

and was doubled up in laughter.)

Language Barrier

When I was small my mother spoke to me
in consonants, flicked them like fag-ends
across the floor to trip me. And I,

tongue-tied, tried to hide from the clicked
disapproval of her *tut tut tut*,
my attempts not to annoy dismissed with *huh*.

Even her silence was sibilant, broken only
when certain words wheezed towards me
tasting the air, hissing a last warning. Now

she is an old woman and her voice
is softening – consonants morph into vowels,
more and more of them lengthening

as that magic 'e' is tagged on, stretching
her speech towards affection – the sharp
uh that once answered my questions

expanding into a long *U*. These days the word
she uses most isn't *I*, it's *You*. It's a mystery.
Was there a moment when my mother's anger

at her difficult child began to evaporate?
Perhaps it happened the day I drove her
to the country to see the crocuses

and she stood, hands loosening a little
on her stick, the only sound she could make
the hushed amazement of the letter O.

Nests

Mary Robinson

The dream loom was broken –
We found some torn Birds nests
she wrote in her journal
the year of her brother's marriage;
one evening he placed the ring
on her finger to wear all night.

The nest is shaped to the bird
as the house to its lovers,
disparate clutter
woven into one piece,
swallows under the rafters
the ultimate symbiosis of nest to house.

I come back to the summer house – it breathes
deeply as I throw open the windows,
children run to the cupboard at the top of the stairs
find toys;
my hands touch once gathered wood clay straw fabric feathers
and stay for a while the unravelling dream.

Such a soft round word
for something at the cutting edge of life
a place
for breeding rearing and parting
where desire irresistible as a magnet
can turn to hate's acid etching out the heart.

The Dunnabeck

David Scott

i. m.   Robert Woof

It began with that picture by Haydon
of Wordsworth in the beck
standing on a rock, thinking through one arm
held at the elbow, indicating
a longish pose. I don't mean any irony.
I like it. I like it intensely because
I would naturally do the same but quicker
or fear of being observed, or snapped into
conversation by 'do you live round here?'

I wander from rock to rock remembering
Robert and thinking what he will be now:
part of the great everything perhaps,
or particular in some particular way
to do with what mattered to him.
And not just books, but his genius
of engaging one with another.

Then there were the rocks, the water and the air,
and the way they speak the truth just enough
and automatically, like the space above,
and all that ragged, shabby clothes stuff…

The Poet   *William Gilson*

The lawnmowered grass by the lake,
green, green; haze: across the water the hills
are grainy with little colored particles.
Trying to remember why I'm
here, sitting on a wooden chair
which is too wide. Has this woman shrunk?
Were her hips that wide?

                    The joke
is this: everyone here is dead, except me.

Well, that is to call myself exceptional,
which I've decided not to do – me, the
greatest living poet. And not a line,
a word, remembered. Me, who always
recited from memory.

                    "If my reason
Will thereto be obedient, I have reason - "

Something tells me that's not mine.

"Now I knew I lost her - not that she was gone - "

That's the little New England mouse kneeling
on her folded towel, gardening,
hiding when company comes.
                              You,
you want poetry, try this -

"Condom, condom, lying low,
where does your water whistle grow - "

Christ, the indignity.

                    Big dark shadow now
coming in low over the water - maybe
Doctor Stealth Bomber Death, O
take me, take me up. Torture me for the
information - make me remember my poems –

then when you're done
drop me from a great height,
my jokes are wearing thin, they are
letting in the true picture, the ordinary
way of saying it. Push me out and
let me fall - snap the membrane - hard,
instant, lights out, like that calm man
in his blue machine.
He went speeding, skimming –
he nearly broke the record!

Heaney at Grasmere

Patricia Pogson

A man with a haircut
like a demented bluebell
introduces the poet.

Restless Americans
take their Collecteds
out of paper bags,
put them in again.

If anyone lights a cigarette
they cough in ruffled protest,
swig mineral water from bottles.

Everybody claps. Though
nobody's done anything. Yet.

An American – from Boston? –
puts his paper bag
under his chair.

The poet reads.
He's folding sheets
with his mother
spotless geometries.

Question Time.
An Oxford don
delivers a statement
he's been rehearsing
for half an hour

The American hawks,
Spits in his paper bag.

Our hands speak thanks.

The poet receives, blesses,
A shuffling line.

The American unfolds forward,
asks the poet to sign
his damp paper bag.

The Over-Stayers

Judy Brown

The bus timetable slims
down in the winter months,
to almost half its size.

Patterdale's gone from the map;
the summer slog
up Kirkstone subtracted,

leaving a slit in the day
like a cutpurse's fraying scar.
The air is something spacious

in these abandoned seasons.
Our breath slows; each swallow
is smoother than the last.

November's a plain meat
after the coach party summer,
glossy with holiday money,

trays of stuck-together chips.
Ambleside, rainy and inadvertent,
casts a half-shut eye.

No bus for hours: we stand
unjostled at the bar,
our stories swelling like clouds.

'Grasmere Lake'   *Emily Hasler*

A tautology, yes, but then the pedant's tut
ignores precisely the fact: some things deserve
the slip of double affirmation, being twice named
for good reason – once for the mere width, once
more for those hidden depths. Gasp not
at the reiteration but the escapology,
the trick by which we entangle further to detach,
the reason for the taut surface and infinite trapdoors
which open only once and promptly close fast.

Teas Maid, Rampsbeck Hotel.

Maggie Reed

The back door is locked.
I'll have to think, quick.
Try the kitchen window – locked.
Go round to the front
(the lake holds its breath).
A sash window in the dining room
moves as I pull. I heave it open,
crouch through, knock a table in passing.
A spoon falls to the floor.

The trays are ready for me.
Number 6 – knock hard,
Number 11 – leave outside the door,
Number 10 – leave till last.
Only three rooms booked midweek
high season, and that view
To die for – but this was before
Tripadvisor. A school holiday job,
giving me something to get up for.

Sometimes they asked me to draw the curtains,
asked how the lake was looking.
Others averted their eyes, pulled white
towelling dressing gowns (with the initials RH)
tight across their chests,
wiped their sleepy eyes, looked
bewildered at the tea tray.

At the end of the shift, after draining
the kitchen sink, pulling marmalade peel
from the plughole, I'd collect my wages,
catch the bus home, go back to bed
for a proper sleep.

rail replacement bus service. *Alan John Stubbs*

the green gleam of leaves turning
metal, fragile, brittle, is changing

as we traverse water that is still
across the road on the way in to Aspatria after

the flood, just a small flood this time
three hundred or so houses emptied out

Oh! but the light is breaking the sky
through a low cloud so forbidding

up high is a blue clear high, and the view
as we descend to the train station by

the Lake District Creamery with it's ageless
sign, a black and white cow and a milk churn -

is of a builders yard with a white van, and the usual
stacks of used wooden pallets

the bus reverses into to turn back
up the road at Johanna Terrace - but what

a light – all encompassing
everything bright as a button

a yellow wagon smiles into reverse letting us on
two horses in a field are waked by the sun

West Street Health Centre stands ablaze
while across the street the Red Lion slumbers in shade

the black faced sheep never looked so clean
electricity pylons are positively gleaming

and the tops of hedges shocked into a last
thrust up in the air

are a child's hair under the influence
of a Van de Graaff Generator

Canal

Alan Forsyth

Day by day the narrow boats go by
And by and by and by and by.
Each one by one and one again they pass,
Passing water from high to lower lock, then
Floating up or down accordingly
To the appropriate level and direction.
They chuffle onward to their destination
Hopefully, but showing little true elation,
Exchanging smiling greetings as they pass
From hence to somewhere else then back.
Still, day by day these gentle boats go by
And by and by and by and by and by.

At Derwentwater

Pat Moneypenny

The children paddled ankle-deep in mud,
And walked their boots clean through the splashy grass,
And ran and shouted down the autumn field,
Above the lake of ribbed and shining glass.

Beneath the tent-eaves shone the harvest moon,
Far brighter than our lamp to end the day;
The purple, rounded mountains, rank on rank,
Now disappeared in shadows far away.

And when the sudden heavy rain lashed down,
We pulled our blankets closer round, and kept
Our eyes fast-closed, and in our snug cocoons
In the long hush-sh-sh of rain we slept.

-To wake in the chill morning air again
To find the whole world sparkling and refreshed –
A clear blue sky, a deep blue lake,
And all the range of mountains gold-enmeshed.

Theatre By The Lake, Keswick   *Anne Middleton*

Haunted by Ibsen's rain
we chill out on
ice-cream and appraise
staging erected for the interval.

The drops are inter-slotted
cut-outs of the fells
stacked in descending blues:
Grisedale the bleached

backcloth. The lowered
sun directs the bank of
lighting from behind
clouds as floorboards float in

liquid bronze. Centre stage:
shapes. A rowing boat,
oars orchestrating the water,
soliloquises among dark currents.

On cue a bell rings
for the next act as
a launch exits (left).

Indian Mynah Bird   *David Bell Nicholson*

At Conishead Priory, on the shore of Morecambe Bay
a hundred miles south-west of the Durham collieries,
there was a miners' convalescent home.

Gunga Din would listen for those lads,
the ones with wind enough
who'd struggle up the street,
thirsty for The Farmers Arms.
At the rattle of the latch
he'd cock his head,
his eyes bright, yellow beak agape.

He'd shake his dusky feathers out,
leap around from perch to perch:
Haway, canny lads, he'd crow.
Us boozers always laughed.
The Durham fellas grinned,
gasped: *Haway spuggy marra*,
from their coal-caked lungs.

When the men were gone,
who'd dug as far beneath the waves
as Bardsea is from Morecambe –
rocks and sands and all that weight
of water overhead,
the home closed down.

Yet still the locals risked a smile
as Gunga hacked and hawked
and asked: *What are yer 'avin pet?*
and called the bar-maid *Bonny Lass*
and coughed and coughed as if
his breast were clagged with dust.

Digging at Burnside Court, Carlisle *John Irving Clarke*

Digger

a generic term for bulldozers,
tractors, car-carriers or anything
with big wheels.

The wheels we use now
track us through the stifling
heat of Burnside Court.

With the safety brake on
we sit in the conservatory and watch
two high-vis jacketed workers

fingerless-gloved and woolly hat-
protected against the wind
which slices like a blade.

They are building a garden extension
promising enhanced
sensory perception,

digging, sifting and laying down blocks,
caught in the tiger stripe strobe
of winter sun through trees.

Now I sip on tea and how
parental approval is won
by making a good strong cuppa.

A tipper truck negotiates deep trenches
delivering its black topsoil load…

…*Digger.*

My father polishes this nugget
unearthed from the trove
of memory.

Digger.
Family lore insists
this was my first word.

But I can't believe it wasn't mam,
or, when he came in
from work on the railway,

what he called
his daily walk to London
and back,

it wasn't
another word for Dad.

Spirit level

Jo Stoney

Long as my father's forearm
a solid block of weathered oak
with brass fittings, pitted with age;
one skylight window, one porthole,
holding neon tubes, each floating
a precise bubble, like cod-liver-oil
capsules, the impossible trick
was always to balance both
between narrow grey lines-
stability in two dimensions.

Saturday morning; I am in his garage
sorting tools for my mother.
She is upstairs on the wrong side
of the bed, packing pyjamas, jackets
into Oxfam bags. Forty years ago
I spent weekends planing timber,
or under the bonnet while he passed
spanners, read aloud from Haynes,
translating diagrams of
head gaskets, distributor caps.
He taught me to measure
the smallest gaps, and
how never to be afraid of
taking something to pieces.

Now I choose from his shelves,
what to keep and what to put
in a car boot sale; the battered
biscuit tin of nuts and bolts,
a brand new set of washers,
four shillings and sixpence,
this weighty spirit level
with its yellow unsettled eyes.
Bending to the cold concrete floor
I can feel his hand steadying my elbow.

Broken Biscuits

Kathleen Jones

Aunt Hilda was a packer at the biscuit works
sorting the custard creams and plain digestives
bringing us bags of crumbed fragments
that tasted of each other, dipped in a hot brew.
The teapot was glazed with tannin inside
and out, its bitter tang offset with reject pink-
iced fancies. When Hilda cuddled me I wriggled
free from the tight press of her arms and the need
I sensed at five or six but couldn't name; told
my mother that I loathed the odour of vanilla.

Hilda was late-married to my uncle Fred, a nervy
mother's boy, marched to the church door – we were
told – by brothers of the bride he never made
a wife. She wept daily at her sister's kitchen table;
broke open on the bus to Blackpool screaming that
God would make her pregnant with the child
she longed for. Sectioned to the Bedlam
we were all afraid of, bare rooms that stank of urine
and singed hair, Hilda, shocked into sanity but altered,
walked with us in the garden, quiet with blank eyes.

Fred was obsessed with cleanliness, feared
germs, contamination; wouldn't shake your hand.
And when he sickened like a child she fed him
with a spoon, nursed him, washed his clothes
winding him into the sheet she hoped
would be his last. She found release among
the company of women on the packing line
fattened on that sweet diet, smelling of chocolate
and vanilla, consuming the crumbs, never the whole thing.

Sheila

Ayelet McKenzie

Sheila is in charge
of the bins,
refuse and recycling.
She knows the days when
they have to come out,
and the times they have
to be dragged back in.
She will supervise the bins
of laggard neighbours,
who have relapsed
through error or sin.

Once she shrieked
in the sea's waves
with girlfriends in December,
asked the barman
at the local dive
to turn the music up,
where she danced, wrecked her hair
until the early hours of morning.

My Niece shouts Wh-hoo and
the big Boys & Girls don't matter.   *Emma McGordon*

For Aimee

You teach me more in this moment
than I will show you in a lifetime.

It's early Autumn and the skatepark is framed
by jackets elbowed off around its edges,
their linings curved in the shape they landed
to look like giant luminous snail shells
on the black tarmac against yellowing grass.

The air, thin as a stretched line
between home time and sunset,
is pegged with the sounds of a school-night,
and the hills look purple in the distance.
It's twenty past six and the street lamps catch
tells me that the earth is turning.

You are the only girl here and much younger,
your skinny legs, furious with the pedals
on a bike you'll soon be too big for, are egg shell brown.
I am stood standing holding your pink coat
as though I still have hold of your hand,
tensing my grip when you wobble.

The older boys do tricks,
bump fists in complicated patterns,
and the girls, when they come,
a gang in the dusk distance, loiter
like pink limbed geese, goose bumps
on the backs of their arms folded across their chests
like the shame of clipped wings.

You don't see them
or take mind of the boys you weave,
or me, or notice when the geese leave
under the last streak of gold in the sky,
because you are a lone song sparrow,
whose song, in the late September air, is wh-hoo, wh-hoo, wh-hoo.

School Holiday

Ayelet McKenzie

As they were bored with their leisure
we took the neighbours' children to the sea;
where the sand is striped with mussel shell,
dark blue black, gritty,
like stubble on an unshaven chin.
On the beach lay the carcass of a sheep;
the boys stoned it, to kill it some more,
then kicked savagely at an empty oil drum.
Further on they found a dead jellyfish,
squashy yet firm, like an octopuses eye,
they stoned that too.
Joanne touched it and shivered.

Ginny

Kathleen Jones

The brothers
swill the farm dirt
from their torsos
at the kitchen sink
and sit at table
watching their sister
lift the heavy silver pot
to pour the tea.

Embroidered hollyhocks and roses frame
the text upon the parlour wall.
'Christ is the Head of this House
The Invisible Guest at every meal.'

Ginny carves the bread against her breast
dealing the slices to her brothers
seeing her father's shadow at their backs
putting her school prize on the fire.

The parlour clock ticks away the unused time.
Hollyhocks smother the window's light
to a green dusk.
Ginny smooths her grey reflection
in the teapot's face
passing her brothers the cake
without a word.

Christmas at Goosemire Farm

Gary Liggett

It was Christmas Eve,
wind-blown snow cosied
misted windows.
Bess lay expectantly by the hearth,
and so we began decking
the tree with plump berries
teasels, holly, oranges
brightly lit tallows,
and the flickering fire
made me think of clapcake,
so I said: "clapcake would be nice,"
and he said: "yes, clapcake
with a dollop of apple jelly;
so I went into the scullery,
and it takes a few minutes
to make clapcakes
and I did not know
if he wanted dripping
or fresh butter,
and when I came out
to ask him, he held a puppy,
just like that, in the time
it took me to think,
dripping or butter;
our Bess started whelping,
right beside the warm fire.

Wolf Moon in Leo, 2018

Dry Stone Wall

Dickon Abbott

Once, the barricades of change:

bones of the mountain,
pulled from scars
that mark its side

and laid in lines
like butchers' marks,
to parcel out the land.

Thus each small king could claim
his patch, to feast on: nature
enclosed, under new management.

But your strength outlived their passing,
and the earth's green spreading skin
reclaimed you for itself.

Now you stand, pointing our way up fells,
as outstretched cairns to walk by,
only a signature of lives that held,

brittle yet tenacious as bracken,
to this valleyside, burying
their hopes in its soil.

And when you fall we'll send out
ambulances of cheerful volunteers
who'll mend the limbs with love.

This afternoon, above the valley roar,
in late September sun, your lichened side
imprints, like braille, its message into mine:

Don't just do something – stand there.

Gapping

Mike Smith

The stone wall's down.
Twelve feet of it are gone
And Jimmy's sheep are in.
They're on the lawn,
A garden party crowd.

I say I've never built a wall.
Keep it browd, he says. That's all.

Norman Nicholson's old poem
Reminds me how to grow
It with my gardener's hand.

The stones show me the rest.
Rock shaking heads when wrong,
Settle and lock where they belong.

I build it like a poem, to stand.

Layering

Kathleen Swann

It was a Sunday   which meant
nothing when the day was sweet
and the hedge needed laying
he held no truck with tractors
tearing tender spears raw   dripping sap
through spikes of twigs frayed like torn cloth.

He says the skill is in the eye
not in the strength of an arm
a cut in the right place laid to the sun
gives the pleacher new life to be
tomorrow's stem for flower and fruit
let wildlife pass through the smeuse.

The tools had been his fathers
each one hanging   oiled and sharp
on carefully aligned hooks in the shed
battle ready   glinting in the light
waiting for the heavy dew to lift
with the skylarks in early warmth.

He lays his hands gently along
the hawthorn trunk measuring
the right height to place the cut
the shape of his father's fingers
dented in the handle   the billhook
falls through the air   startling sparrows.

Dead art

Pauline Yarwood

Someone round here has a sense of humour —
the fox, not noticeably damaged,
placed on a mossy bank
with its forelegs crossed in repose,
as though waiting for afternoon tea

and further along the lane a dead badger
lies along the top of a thicket hedge,
sitting up slightly, with its legs wrapped round,
hugging the telegraph pole,
as though it could save him.

Aftermath, Kendal

Debbie Mayes

Stream becomes sea,
road becomes river,
homes become unsafe harbours,
belongings bob like boats.

New moon tiptoes between heaving clouds
lighting up houses and lives turned inside out,
wooden gates hang limply askew, garden walls pushed outside
in.
White goods line the pavements as if waiting for a funeral to
pass.

On the Waterside, weeds are wrapped around railings,
eerie tributes to what is lost.

Gote Bridge, Cockermouth, 5-8 December 2015*

Hilary Tattershall

Over there some lights were on.
Before the rain-shrouded day faded
we could see that we were
marooned in glass and steel,
lapped by a moat from the river.
We all partied by torchlight and
wore our coats to stop the shivering.

Yesterday, two days later, lights
blazed on the other side. The water
had slipped away and left its mark
on the walls of our fortress.
Beneath the bridge a tree's corpse
clunked on the current against the arch,
holding back bushes and weed.

Today Christmas lights in town
glowed; our power came back too,
so I could see to empty the freezer.
I tried to go over to buy milk and bread.
"You cross at your own risk,"
said a policeman on guard over
mud-soaked furniture and TVs.

*Storm Desmond ravaged Cumbria and flooded Cockermouth
again*

Grange-Over-Sands, 2027 *Maggie Reed*

In the second week the Bay search and rescue team
located the clock tower. As the waters settled
to the new high tide, the promenade
became an underwater playground
for flukes, crabs and shrimp.
The abandoned lido had never been so full;
sea water two metres above the parapets,
graffiti collaged with seaweed.

The divers went in on the third week.
Those who'd stayed on long swept away;
no bodies but bottles floating in lines
from the Commodore Hotel. Beer pipes rinsed,
crisp packets still in their boxes salvaged.
A huddle of walking boots launched from Lancaster Shoes,
washed up in the church porch alongside a sodden sock.
Butterfingers freezer was still on the blink.

The post office counter, swept clean of forms,
an echo of *next please*, but there was no queue.
The tides subsided, rooftops shone bright,
stripped of their mosses, choked chimneys
belched trapped air. The roundabout by the Crown
was the first road to appear, the following Thursday
you reached the station in your wellington boots.
The ornamental pond was more or less intact.

On the morning of the fifth we saw the edge of town,
black iron railings rimming the tide,
saw that the river had changed its path,
flowed close to the Prom over the salt marsh,
so boats could return bringing rescuers, workers;
no need for the Queen's Guide to the Sands[1].

The pool remained full, perfect for swimming.
It took a tsunami, but we got our lido back.

---

[1]The Queen's Guide to the Sands is the royally appointed guide to crossing the sands of
Morecambe Bay, an ancient and potentially dangerous tidal crossing in northwest England

Sea Change

Maggie Norton

River Crake crawls from Coniston reeds,
  licks his hunger at the feet of yellow flag,
    bellies out to Allen Tarn.
      Pauses.

Sprawls lethargic in the midday heat;
  skin flattens in the millpond hush;
    sway of weeds press out
      slow breath.

Damselflies pinned in length like
  sapphires enamel his shimmering face,
    stitch the reeds to fringe his body.
      Skin ripples.

Eels throb their thin pectorals
  thrust power along his flanks,
    ease him over jostling pebbles.
      Force entry.

Cows ignored, he squeezes under
  bridges, slithers into Morecambe Bay,
    swells to a sly serpent lurking.
      Quicksand.

Curlew Calling

John Fox

What would you give for the call of a curlew?

They are leaving us.
Elegant and strong, straw legs long,
bent beaked, oatmeal flecked.
Melancholic tuning forks.

Another way of being.

Leaving us because
we gave them cash crop furrows,
a predation of foxes
and EU crows.

Not often a taxidermist weeps.
But, as she held the curvature of the earth,
beak bent from ancient evolution,
feathers falling,
her fingers fumbled with glass eyes
black and bright as acid.

What would you give for the last call of the last curlew?

Ospreys at Foulshaw Moss

Andrew Forster

Huge nest knitted from deadfall and grass,
the male balanced on the lip like an Emperor,
it's cloud-like body robed in pitch-brown wings
and face masked in black like a raider;
its mate tearing at a fish as if
at any second it could be snatched from her grasp.

The watchers around the telescope are rapt,
gripped by the scene in the crook of a spruce
jutting from the Moss like a ruined tower.
Around us the Reserve is waking with white breaths
of cotton grass, tiny flames of bog asphodel,
and damselflies, electrifying the morning.

Rescued from plans for a landfill site
this place nudges nature the way it wants
to go: uprooting conifers to let it flood,
be the wetland it used to be before
fields were drained; and building a nesting platform
when Ospreys were seen passing over.

We take these things as signs of nature
easing back to health. Once hunted and stuffed
and rare as a Golden Eagle, now the male
is everywhere: perched on a telegraph pole,
winging around Whitbarrow Scar and, once,
diving into the bay, talons forward.

Making Good

Patricia Pogson

Last night wind untidied the village
slicing flowers from hanging baskets.

I walk past. You'd have fetched each one home
to sit in jugs, egg cups.   Expect me
to revive crushed victims. I had to sneak out
the hopeless, hide bodies. You'd drop
a lopped dandelion into the beck
watch it slip under the bridge, wink out of sight,
kick storm-felled branches to the roadside,
lift dead voles, hedgehogs, into long grass.

Clearing a space in chaos
Making it your own.

tidying

Ila Colley

sitting: so tonight while outside the trees
make their tender licks at the storm
as it begins to fray out, stoic
over the villages and becomes just
a blameless pinch of the flat dark, i am
making a name for myself in the bathroom.

striding: there had been a moment at 15:00
an elderly couple at the side of the road
just before the Raise submerges
into the civil obedience of pubs
bike helmets and public bridleways
& tired of the presumptuous pugfaces
of silver cars at 60mph, somebody
was no longer waiting to cross.

sealing: there is a time left running: passenger-seat
sounds sinter the porcelain, drag a body
through the exhibits of this room, pink
me into the walls; where i can observe
these residual irreversibles. plughole haloes
slowly; a long lens bending truth, finally
a sorrow tries on my skin & sense stays
mute, worn flippant as a birthmark.

White Moss Tarn

Ann Miller

See the tall mare's tails
waiting the time to bush.

Slender leaved irises
poised to exhibit yellow heads.

Both have made roots
in a lime coloured bed.

The moss dark
under the water

where upside down
in light grey sky

deep green tree trunks
growing spring leaves, shimmer.

Rain drops into rings
of radiating light.

The grass's edge
mixed with rush and nettle.

The Candlelighter

Simon Armitage

From Dove Cottage I sloped out through the side gate
and climbed the corpse-road past the Coffin Stone,
then curved through a mixed copse to a scree path
scored by rainwater into the hill's back.
I was hauled upwards by a borrowed dog
on a makeshift leash, a yellow Labrador
gunning for every birdcall and blown leaf.
Over a hand-stacked wall, in the next fold,
under the driftwood bones of a late elm
a red deer had dropped down from the fell
with morning beaconed in its flaming horns.
With dawn-light cradled in its branching crown.
I stood in some blind-spot of its dark eye
and deer and dog were still and unaware
and stayed that way, divided by the wall:
wild stag and hunting hound in separate worlds,
before the deer pushed on through tinder thickets,
igniting the next field. And the dog yawned.
Then I hacked up the ghyll to higher ground
counting the hikers striding along the ridge,
thinking of taking a drink from the tarn,
thinking of adding a new stone to the cairn.

Cold Gathering

Polly Atkin

Soft-soled boots   slow moss step
heel-toe roll   shallow tread
stitched to deliberate breath, siphoned
diaphragm to lip.
          I hear them first:
stop my foot mid-curl from its spongy perch.
Star moss.
        Beech shells.
                Cautious crunching.
A small deer nosing at the musty ground
across the clearing.   More here than I am.
This, the autumn's first cold gathering.
I like to snap dry lengths of branch against my shin.
These woods are our closest neighbour. The path
a churning of leaves since a storm mid-week.
I am off-balance.   Negotiating inclination.
Half way up I snare myself thinking
a place of power.
         I hear them first.
The body of the deer is the exact
dim brown of beech-bark at twilight.
It erases itself with studied stillness
in the mouth of the darkening glade   present
in its black eyes' shimmer. Its companion in
background blurred with intention   a fraction
of a turn to gesture the ghost white flag
of its backside.   The two deer stare.   I stare.
They bow their heads.   I bow my head.
I am deer-coloured in my warmest coat, sheep-scented.
They pick on into the baring trees.
         What manner of beast I may be is unsure.

I am alone and particularly quiet.
I am carrying a plastic bag of sticks.
There is power in this opening. In the carved trunks
of the ring of beeches   their ossified dendroglyphs
JD 1964
       I ♥ MY WIFE
             JH BB 1945
the rise from the valley floor. The wood
is our closest neighbour.   It feeds our fire.
I want to go where the deer are going
but I do not want to make them run.
I watch them until I lose them   until
they weave their thin limbs into saplings
and the heron's low familiar sweep
of the field from the house to the river.

Winter Migrants *Tom Pickard*

an animal wakes
when I walk, in winter,

wrapped against
a withering wind,

solitary,

on a Solway flat

a mass of moth-eaten cloud
threadbare and spun across
a bullish moon

winter migrants gather
in long black lines

along a silver sleek

heads held back,
throats
       thrust toward
an onshore rush

occasionally cruciform,
      static
in a flying wind

as though
in obeisance
      to the sea

each tide a season
in the pecking mall

retracing steps
            washed out
by whimpering silt

they call as I approach,
an upright spelk
  on their shelf,

            gathering my notes
and theirs

we scavenge
            ahead of our shadows

waiting for what

the tide brings in
or leaves out

purple,
                hedged cloud
edged gold

                hung
on silver slates
                of sand

diverted
                leaps of light
surrender water

risen
                from rivulets
roughed
                from rage

repealing waves
                repeat

a curlew's
                estuary echo

who,
                but you
        and the wind's
wake?

ACKNOWLEDGEMENTS

DICKON ABBOTT 'Dry Stone Wall' from *The Mark We Make* (Dickon Abbott Estate, 2007); SIMON ARMITAGE 'Untitled' from *New Cemetery*©Simon Armitage and 'The Candlelighter' ©Simon Armitage, first appeared in *The Unaccompanied* (Faber and Faber, 2018) reproduced by permission of Faber and Faber Ltd; POLLY ATKIN 'Cold Gathering' from *Invisible Rain* (New Walk Press Pamphlet, 2018); GRAHAM AUSTIN 'White Horses' from *Morecambe Bay and Local Poets* (2010, Austin G. ed); ALISON BARR 'Screen Lass' from *Honey and Stone, A Collection of Poems by Alison Barr*; ROSS BAXTER 'Turning Left' from *Ten Ways To Fly* (mOOnman, 1984); JOHN IRVING CLARK 'Digging at Burnside Court, Carlisle' an earlier version appeared as 'In a New Word for Dad'; John Irving Clarke's 2016 collection *To Owls* (Currock Press, 2016); JENNIFER COPLEY 'Hartley's Boat' was highly commended in the Mirehouse Prize 2007; NEIL CURRY 'A Quaker Graveyard with Peacocks' from *The Road to Gunpowder House* (Enitharmon, 2003); KERRY DARBISHIRE 'The Earth of Cumberland is my Earth' from *Distance Sweet on my Tongue* (Indigo Dreams, 2018); KATE DAVIS 'Language Barrier' was published in The Poetry School Pamphlet Blueprint as part of the Northern Writers Awards scheme in 2014; HELEN FARISH 'The Old Chancel, Ireby' and 'Judgement Day' from *The Dog of Memory* (Bloodaxe, 2016); ANTOINETTE FAWCETT 'News' - The epigraph is a quotation from *The Flowering Plum and the Palace Lady*: Interpretations of Chinese Poetry, trans. Hans H. Frankel (Yale University Press, 1976); BRIAN FEREDAY 'Fellside Cottage Orchard' from *Homeground* (Fulmus Press, 2015); ALAN FORSYTH 'Canal' was first published in *Time and Tide* (Alan Forsyth, 2018); JOHN FOX 'Curlew Calling' in *Curlew Calling* (Ed. Karen Lloyd, 2017); GILL FRANCES. 'Keswick Museum' was 'Highly Commended' in the 2016 Mirehouse Poetry Competition; HARRIET FRASER 'Gaps in the Duddon Valley'- An edited version published in *Land Keepers* (somewhere-nowhere press, 2014) and 'Ethnography' Journal, 2015; GERALDINE GREEN 'I used to know these things' from *Salt Road* (Indigo Dreams, 2013); KATIE HALE 'Offcomer' was shortlisted for the 2017 Frogmore Poetry Prize and subsequently published in the Frogmore Papers: Issue 90 (Sep.2017); EMILY HASLER 'Grasmere Lake' from Emily Hasler, *The Built Environment* (Liverpool University Press, 2018) and reproduced with permission; GEOFFREY HOLLOWAY 'Long Meg and Her Daughters' and 'Lazarus' from Collected Poems (Arrowhead, 2007); PHIL HOUGHTON 'Alpine' appeared on the Flora of the Fells project website; KATHLEEN JONES 'Ginny' from *Not Saying Goodbye at Gate 21* (Templar Poetry, 2011), 'Broken Biscuits' from *The Emma Press Anthology of Aunts* (Emma Press, 2017); NICOLA JACKSON 'Reading Rooms' from *Crossing the Wild* (North Cumbria Poetry Society Stanza Anthology, 2017); CHRIS KELLY 'Humphrey Head' from *Next Door to Paradise. Poems from Low Furness* (2009); SUE KINDON 'The Heart Shaped Wood' appeared in February 2018 on the blog *Bonnie's Crew*, a site set up by Kate Garrett to raise money for the Children's Heart Surgery Fund; SARAH LITTLEFEATHER DEMICK 'My Shepherd' from *Another Creature* (Sarah Littlefeather Demick); CAROLA LUTHER 'St. Oswald's Church Grasmere' from *Walking the Animals* (Carcanet, 2004) by kind permission of the author and publisher. Also from a collaborative project by the Lakes Collective (2013); AYELET McKENZIE 'Sheila' published in *Small Bear* (Caterpillar Poetry); KIM MOORE 'Walney Channel' and 'Sometimes you think of Bowness' from *If We Could Speak Like Wolves* by Kim Moore (Smith/Doorstop Books, 2012); HELEN MORT 'Coffin Path' and 'The Dogs' from *Division Street* by Helen Mort. Published by Chatto and Windus, 2013. Copyright ©Helen Mort. Reproduced by permission of the author c/o Rogers, Coleridge and White Ltd., Powis Mews, London W11 1JN; MAGGIE NORTON 'Sea Change' from *Onions and Other Intentions* (Indigo Dreams, 2012); M.R.PEACOCKE 'The Vegetable Catalogue', first published (under a different title) in *Speaking of the Dead* (Peterloo Poets, 2003); TOM PICKARD 'Winter Migrants' from *Winter Migrants*, Tom Pickard (Carcanet, 2016) by kind permission of the author and publisher; CHRIS PILLING 'Wordsworth for a Local' from *Coming Ready or Not* (Bookcase, 2009) and 'Sessile Oak' from *Tree Time* (Redbeck, 2003); PATRICIA POGSON 'Making Good' from *Holding* (Flambard, 2002) and 'Heaney at Grasmere' from *The Tides in the Basin* (Flambard, 1994); JACOB POLLEY 'Jackself's Hymn' and 'The Snow Prince' © Jacob Polley by kind permission of the author; EILEEN PUN - an earlier version of 'When the Subject of Our Childhoods Came Up' was published in *Birdbook III Anthology*, Edited by Kirsten Irving & Jon Stone (Sidekick Books, 2015); MAGGIE REED 'Grange-over-Sands, 2027' also in The North magazine (North 60, August 2018); MARY ROBINSON 'Nests' first published in Mary Robinson *The Art of Gardening* (Flambard Press, 2010); DAVID SCOTT 'St Herbert's Isle', *Derwentwater from Beyond the Drift* (Bloodaxe, 2014) with the kind permission of the publishers; ALAN JOHN STUBBS 'Unable to see the Sheila Fell Landscape' and 'rail replacement bus service' from 'tomorrow is the tugboat of today' (The Onslaught Press, 2018).

THE POETS

Dickon Abbot was born in Sussex in 1962 into a family of five boys. He studied History at Lincoln College, Oxford. He moved to the Lake District in 1986 and followed a career in social work. He died on 23rd February 2004 and was buried in the Quaker burial ground in Ulverston.

Ina Anderson grew up in Barrow-in-Furness and Kirkby-in-Furness. Though she now lives in Vermont, in the USA, she returns to Cumbria every year. Her poetry collection, *Journey Into Space,* was published by Antrim House in 2017. Royalton Radio in Vermont regularly broadcasts her poetry radio show, Wordstream.

Simon Armitage, born in West Yorkshire, is Professor of Poetry at the University of Oxford. He has published eleven collections of poetry, including *Seeing Stars* (2010), *Paper Aeroplane: Selected Poems 1989–2014* (2014), *The Unaccompanied* (2017) and has published a translation of *Sir Gawain and the Green Knight* (2007). He writes for television and radio; is the author of two novels and the non-fiction bestsellers *All Points North* (1998), *Walking Home* (2012) and *Walking Away* (2015). He has read yearly at the Wordsworth Trust in Grasmere for 22 years.

Polly Atkin lives in Grasmere. Her first poetry collection, *Basic Nest Architecture* (Seren, 2017) followed pamphlets *Bone Song* (Aussteiger, 2008) (shortlisted for the Michael Marks Pamphlet Award, 2009) and *Shadow Dispatches* (Seren, 2013) (Mslexia Pamphlet Prize winner, 2012). Her most recent pamphlet is *With Invisible Rain* (New Walk Press, 2018). She is a Penguin Random House Write-Now mentee, for a forthcoming non-fiction book reflecting on place, belonging and chronic illness.

Graham Austin (1938-2015) was born in Kent, formed on Tyneside, and a college lecturer in Ipswich, before moving to Morecambe Bay with his wife Sandra where he became a published poet. He was a regular performer and attender at A Poem and a Pint events in Cumbria, and a founder-member of A Posse of Poets from Furness.

Anne Banks has had poems performed on stage locally and published in Orbis and assorted national anthologies. She has attended many writing workshops and completed two poetry writing courses on Lancaster University's outreach programme. She is currently a member of Writers' Rump and Brewery Poets.

Alison Barr was born in Edinburgh and has lived in Spain, France and Australia, as well as remote locations in the West Coast of Scotland. She has now settled in Cumbria. Alison enjoys hiking, science, wildlife, rowing, strong coffee and writing about nature, landscape and life in general.

Ross Baxter has lived for the past 45 years on the same farm at the foot of Coniston Water. A retired teacher and farmer, his writing includes poetry, songs, and plays.

Judy Brown lived in Bowness as a teenager and went to the Lakes School. She was Poet-in-Residence at the Wordsworth Trust during 2013. Her books are *Crowd Sensations* (Seren, 2016), a Poetry Book Society Recommendation and shortlisted for the Ledbury Forte Prize, and *Loudness* (Seren, 2011) which was shortlisted for the Forward and Aldeburgh first collection prizes. www.judy-brown.co.uk

Mark Carson is an offshore engineer, now securely anchored on the shoreline of Morecambe Bay. He writes about the ocean and engineering, business and pleasure, East Africa and Donegal and a whole lot else. His pamphlet *Hove-to is a State of Mind* is published by Wayleave Press (2015).

Alison Carter lives in Cockermouth and has been writing poetry for ten years. She has an MA from MMU and has been mentored at the Wordsworth Trust. She won the 2016 and 2018 Mirehouse Poetry Prize, the 2017 Wordsworth Birthday Prize, and was placed second in the Segora International Competition in 2017.

Antony Christie is now more often in the North Pennines or the highlands of Grey County, after 15 years around Barrow. His poetry has been published in England, Canada and Ireland, and when he's not working with wood or mortar, he writes, assesses student drama, gives readings, or looks for a home for two collections and a chapbook.

John Irving Clarke was born in Carlisle and had his love for writing nurtured in Mrs. Procter's class at Goodwin School. His reading demands were met at Tullie House library and his affiliation to Carlisle United was forged by watching Hugh McIlmoyle. A creative writing tutor, John lives with his wife in Wakefield.

Christine Cochrane is from Scotland and has lived in Cumbria since 1980. She began writing after retiring from teaching, and is currently completing a poetry collection as part of an MA with the Open University. She is a Mslexia short story prizewinner and the author of *Shifting Sands* (Lumphanan Press, 2016).

Ila Colley is originally from the Lake District and has recently graduated from the University of Edinburgh with a degree in Architecture. She won the Foyle Young Poets award in 2013 and 2014. Her work has been published in Ambit, Butcher's Dog, hotdog and The London Magazine online.

Jennifer Copley lives in Barrow with her sculptor husband, her cantankerous cat and rescue greyhound. She has published 3 full collections of poetry and 6 pamphlets, the most recent being *Some Couples* (Happenstance, 2017). She recently won the Cinnamon Pamphlet Collection Prize: *Being Haunted* will be published in 2019.

Felicity Crowley was born in Devon in 1949 and now lives in Cockermouth, surrounded by two children and four grandchildren. A retired teacher, she is involved in the local Green Party, gardening, green woodwork, fell walking and writing about it all.

Neil Curry is a poet, translator and literary critic specializing in 18th century poetry. He has translated plays by Euripides for BBC TV and works by the French poet, Jules Supervielle. His *Selected Poems* were published by Enitharmon Press. His most recent collection *On Keeping Company with Mrs. Woolf* was published by Shoestring Press in 2018.

Duncan Darbishire was born in Penny Bridge, lives just outside of Ulverston, and is a retired doctor, busy gardener, and part time photographer and poet.

Kerry Darbishire lives on a Cumbrian fellside where most of her poetry is rooted. She has won many prizes, including being short-listed for Bridport 2017, and her poems have appeared widely in magazines and anthologies. Her first poetry collection, *A Lift of Wings,* was published by Indigo Dreams in 2014. *Kay's Ark,* the story of her mother, was published by Handstand Press in 2016. Her second poetry collection, *Distance Sweet on my Tongue* (IDP) was published in Autumn 2018.

Kate Davis is a poet from Barrow-in-Furness. Her poems have been published in Iota and Butcher's Dog, implanted in audio-benches, sung through a tide cycle, and printed on shopping bags. In 2013 she received a Northern Writers Award. Her first collection *The Girl Who Forgets How to Walk* is published by Penned in the Margins.

Kelly Davis was born in London, lives in Maryport and works as a freelance editor. Her poems have been published in Mslexia magazine and SpeakEasy magazine and anthologised in P*oetry for Performance* (The Playing Space), *Write to Be Counted* (The Book Mill), Diversifly (Fair Acre Press) and *Dusk* (Arachne Press).

Josephine Dickinson has published four collections of poetry: *Scarberry Hill* (The Rialto, 2001), *The Voice* (Flambard, 2003), *Silence Fell* (Houghton Mifflin, 2007) and *Night Journey* (Flambard, 2008). She lives on a small hill farm in Cumbria.

Ruby Evans was born in Carlisle, Cumbria in 2001. She was one of the 2017 winners of the Poetry Society's 'Foyle Young Poets' competition and was longlisted for the 2018 Christopher Tower Poetry Competition. She is one of the organisers of the Carlisle Poetry Symposium.

Helen Farish has published three collections: *Intimates* (2005), which won the Forward Prize for Best First Collection, *Nocturnes at Nohant* (2012) and *The Dog of Memory* (2016). Her work has also been short-listed for the T.S Eliot Prize and been awarded a Poetry Book Society Recommendation. For further information see www.helenfarish.co.uk.

Antoinette Fawcett lives in Ulverston, Cumbria. After a career teaching English in the UK and abroad, she now works as a literary translator. *Bird Cottage*, her translation of Eva Meijer's *Het Vogelhuis*, will appear in August 2018 with Pushkin Press. Her poems and translations have been published in MPT, Poetry London, Poetry Review, Agenda and Stand, amongst others.

Brian Fereday (1950-2016) was born in the South Cumbrian village of Levens. His early passion for plants, woods and wildlife led to a career in woodland research and forestry. For the last 15 years of his life he wrote poetry inspired by his love of the local countryside. His collection *Homeground* was published by Fulmus Press in 2015.

Andrew Forster has published three books of poetry; *Fear of Thunder*, shortlisted for the Forward Prize for Best First Collection in 2008, *Territory* (both Flambard), and *Homecoming* (Smith Doorstop), shortlisted for the Lakeland Book of the Year Award in 2015. He has worked in Literature Development for 20 years, including 7 years as Literature Officer at the Wordsworth Trust in Grasmere, and runs a number of projects; including the Michael Marks Awards for Poetry Pamphlets and, as co-editor, the online poetry magazine *The Compass*. He is currently finishing a PhD on Poetry and Environmentalism at MMU, where he also teaches as an Associate Lecturer.

Alan Forsyth was born in Cheshire in 1927 and studied art in Liverpool. He worked first for Supermarine as technical Illustrator followed by a variety of engineering companies until joining Furmanite in Cumbria in 1967. He is a writer, painter and freelance illustrator. His poems have been published by University of Wales Publications, *Agni, Aeroplane, Bookcase*, (Highway) Hayloft Press, (Waypoints) Titus Wilson, (Time &Tide). He was a trustee of Brewery Arts Centre, Grizedale, Hadfield Trust and Lancaster University Public Arts Policy and Court.

Juliet Fossey writes poetry which draws from the Cumbrian landscape, often using familiar locations, plants and animals as a foil to explore the issues Cumbrians face living in and around the National Park. Her work includes collaborative projects with artists and musicians to produce video and live performance incorporating written or spoken word.

John Fox MBE has lived in Cumbria for four decades. From 1968-2006 he directed Welfare State International, the celebratory arts company. A radical artist, thinker, performer, printmaker and poet he now works (with Sue Gill) as Dead Good Guides. His work is in several anthologies. www.deadgoodguides.co.uk, www.welfare-state.org.

Gill Frances retired to Cumbria in 2004 after a career spent in teaching. She currently runs the Cumbrian Poets group, begun by Chris Pilling in Keswick nearly forty years ago. Gill also organises the Creative Writing group for the local U3A.

Harriet Fraser has lived in Cumbria since 1995 – a 'short stay' lengthened and, two children and more than twenty years later, Cumbria is most definitely home. Poetry forms part of her work exploring the nature and culture of place. She collaborates with her partner, photographer Rob Fraser, through their practice 'some-where-nowhere'.

Caroline Gilfillan's collection *Yes* won the East Anglian Book Award for the best poetry collection in 2010. Her collection *Pepys* was developed into a performance piece. Her most recent book is *Poet in Boots*. She also writes fiction and songs, and lives in Ulverston. www.carolinegilfillan.co.uk

William Gilson is an American living permanently in Kendal. His novella, *At the Dark End of the Street,* appeared in New England Review. His chapbook of poems, *Monkey Puzzle,* is published by Wayleave. He is co-author, with the photographer Thomas E. Gilson, of *Carved in Stone,* a study of early New England gravestone carving (Wesleyan University Press, 2012).

Ann Grant is a Barrovian living in Kendal. Her writing has appeared on sonic benches, restaurant walls and collaboration albums. She's half of the music duo 2 Baa Chords. She is excited to be in this Cumbrian anthology and to be included with so many poets that she admires.

Geraldine Green is a Cumbrian writer, tutor and poetry editor. She has 3 collections, *The Other Side of the Bridge, Salt Road* and *Passing Through,* Indigo Dreams Publishing Ltd. Her work has been widely anthologised in the UK and US. In 2011, she gained a PhD in Creative Writing Poetry, from Lancaster University.

Katie Hale's debut pamphlet, *Breaking the Surface,* was published by Flipped Eye in 2017. She recently won the Jane Martin Poetry Prize and the Ware Poetry Prize, and her poetry has been published in Poetry Review, The North and Interpreter's House. She is currently working on her first novel.

Emily Hasler lived in Grasmere from 2008 to 2009, while she was intern at the Wordsworth Trust. She now lives on the Essex-side of the river Stour. She has been a Hawthornden Fellow and received an Eric Gregory Award. Her collection, *The Built Environment* is published by Pavilion Poetry (2018).

Tony Hendry was brought up in Workington and Cockermouth. After a civil service career in London, he now lives in Carlisle and is active in its lively poetry scene. He is a late starter whose poems have been published in numerous magazines, including The North and Acumen.

Deborah Hobbs lives and works in Cumbria. She gained an MA in Creative Writing from the Manchester School of Writing. Her poems have been published in several anthologies (Vanguard Editions, Harestone Press).

Hannah Hodgson has been published in The North, Acumen and Under the Radar magazines. She has won a number of competitions organised by the Poetry Society. Her first poetry pamphlet, *Dear Body* explores her illness and disability. She also has a YouTube channel where she discusses poetry, fiction and illness. www.youtube.com/c/HannahHodgson.

Geoffrey Holloway (1918-1997) was one of the most distinctive voices in 20th century British poetry, with an astonishing ear for the music and movement of language. He began to publish poems nationally as early as 1946 but was also intensely active in the small press scene for many decades.

Andy Hopkins has taught in London and Carlisle. His work has appeared in The North, The Interpreter's House, Under the Radar and Southlight. His chapbooks include *Dark Horse Pictures* (Selkirk Lapwing Press, 2007). He was poetry editor for SpeakEasy Magazine (Vol. II) and he runs the Carlisle Poetry Symposium.

Phil Houghton's work, influenced by landscape, is published in Other Poetry, magazines, anthologies, and was performed by Theatre by the Lake, Keswick. A member of Cumbrian Poets, and a Patron of Norman Nicholson Society's Nicholson House project. His poem 'Blencathra' features in Terry Abraham's *Life of a Mountain*, broadcast on BBC4.

Jackie Huck has always written, first in post-war Lancashire. Forty years ago, she moved to Cumbria, where she has been inspired by the tumbling fells, lakes and open skies. She has had two poetry books published and a novel about nursing cadets.

Em Humble grew up in Kendal, and in 2015 joined Dove Cottage Young Poets. She studies English Literature at the University of Leeds where she writes poetry, comedy and screenplays. Her poetry was shortlisted for the Alison Morland Prize and published in The North.

Jonathan Humble is a deputy head teacher in Cumbria. His poetry and short stories have appeared in a number of publications online, in print and on the radio. He regularly performs at Verbalise in The Brewery Arts Centre, Kendal.

Irvine Hunt was born in Lancashire. Following a career in journalism, he moved to Cumbria, where he has been writing poems, stories and photographic histories for over 30 years. His novels *The Drover's Boy* and *The Ghost Show* are published by Handstand Press.

Nicola Jackson has a doctorate in neuroscience. Her poetry is published in newspapers, journals and anthologies. Her debut collection, *Difficult Women*, with Indigo Dreams Press, won the Geoff Stevens Memorial Prize 2017. She has an MA in Writing Poetry and co-edited the human rights anthology *Write To Be Counted*.

Kathleen Jones was born and brought up on a hill farm near Caldbeck and is a poet, novelist and biographer, currently living in an old mill in the Eden valley. Her published work includes 2 novels, 4 collections of poetry, and biographies of Katherine Mansfield, Norman Nicholson, Catherine Cookson and the women of the Wordsworth and Coleridge families.

Chris Kelly was born in 1947, in St Helens Lancashire. She wrote her first poems as an entomology student at Glasgow University. She worked in Africa and lived in Sweden before moving to London to work in journalism (Chris Stretch). She has lived in Bardsea since 1992. Her self-published pamphlet, *Next Door to Paradise,* came out in 2009.

Sue Kindon lived in East Cumbria for nearly 30 years and was a member of Brewery Poets, Kendal. She now lives and writes in The Pyrenees, where she co-runs Valier Illustrated Books. Her first pamphlet, *She Who Pays the Piper*, is available from Three Drops Press.

Charlie Lambert was born in Troutbeck Bridge, raised in Windermere, and went on to work for the BBC as a sports broadcaster. His love of poetry is evidenced not just by his own work but by his role as chair of the Millom-based Norman Nicholson Society. He lives in Liverpool.

Gary Liggett is an English film-maker, writer and poet. His work is held in permanent collections, including the Museum of Modern Art in New York. Influences include: Jim Harrison, Varlam Shalamov, Leonard Cohen, Ken Loach and David Lean. He lives sustainably on a Cumbrian smallholding with his wife and family.

Sarah Littlefeather Demick is an Ojibwa Indian. She was born in Toronto, Canada, and raised by adopted parents in London, England. She works as a carer, lived in Cumbria for 17 years and is married to a musician. They have two dogs and sometimes perform as a folk duo.

Karen Lloyd writes creative non-fiction, poetry and journalism. Her first book, *The Gathering Tide; A Journey Around the Edgelands of Morecambe Bay* (Saraband, 2016) was one of the Observer's top books of 2016 and won the Striding Edge Productions Prize for Place at The Lakeland Book of the Year Awards. *The Blackbird Diaries – A Year with Wildlife*, (Saraband 2017) won the Bookends Arts and Literature Prize in 2018 at The Lakeland Book of the Year Awards. Her poetry has been published in *Reliquiae Volume 5* (Corbel Stone Press) and in *Zoomorphic*.

Angela Locke is the author of seven books, four poetry collections and the film script *In the Mind of Man*. Many of her books are set in Cumbria. She holds an MA in Creative Writing, tutors Mungrisdale Writers, and leads International Creative Writing Retreats. Details of Angela's work are on her website at www.angelalocke.co.uk.

Carola Luther has 2 collections of poems *Walking the Animals* (Carcanet, 2004), *Arguing with Malarchy*, (Carcanet, 2011) and a pamphlet, *Herd*, published in 2012 by The Wordsworth Trust.

Debbie Mayes has lived in Kendal for the last 10 years and her surroundings inform her poetry. She has attended poetry workshops with Janni Howker and two of her poems appear in the anthology *Words for Wellbeing* (edited by Carol Ross).

Emma McGordon was born in Whitehaven and considers Cockermouth to be the place she found home. She is a former Northern Young Writer of the Year and also a recipient of the Julia Darling Fellowship, both from New Writing North. She is published by Penned in the Margins and Tall Lighthouse and a number of anthologies and magazines. She works as a writer, performer and educator.

Ayelet McKenzie came to Barrow 32 years ago after growing up in Leeds. Her poems have appeared in many magazines, including The London Magazine. Her published collections include *The Patient is Disappointing* (Tidefall Press), *Waiting for an Angel* (Selkirk Lapwing Press), *Courting The Asylum* (Survivors Press), *Small Bear* (Caterpillar Poetry), and *Messages Written on Envelope Backs* (Dempsey & Windle).

Anne Middleton studied English at Durham and after twelve housemoves, along with babies and medical librarianship and the magistracy filling her waking hours, is now retired in Kendal, where she has had time to enjoy writing poetry - very slowly!

Ann Miller began life in the North East of England. She attended Hartlepool College of Art, where she was awarded the National Diploma in Design and also worked as a part time teacher. She moved to Cumbria in 1979, continued to paint and is a founding member of the Mungrisdale Writers.

Pat Moneypenny was born in Manchester and lived there for 50 years. She learned to love poetry at school and began writing her own verse at the age of eleven. Following her marriage and birth of two children she moved with her husband to Ulverston where she intends to remain!

Kim Moore's first collection, *The Art of Falling,* was published by Seren in 2015 and won the Geoffrey Faber Memorial Prize. Her pamphlet, *If We Could Speak Like Wolves,* won the 2011 Poetry Business Pamphlet Competition. She lives in Barrow-in-Furness and is currently a PhD candidate at Manchester Metropolitan University.

Helen Mort has published two collections with Chatto & Windus, *Division Street* (2013) and *No Map Could Show Them* (2016). She is a lecturer in Creative Writing at Manchester Metropolitan University. From 2010-11, Helen was Poet in Residence at The Wordsworth Trust, Grasmere.

David Bell Nicholson was born in Ulverston in 1943 and died there in 2013. He taught Art and English, and later, in behavioural special needs. He left behind a wealth of poetry, winning a prestigious prize in the Edinburgh Art Galleries' unpublished poets competition. His poems are in preparation for publication.

Gill Nicholson was born in 1936. In 1999 the BBC and West Yorkshire Playhouse performed her plays. A memoir *The Mirror Game* followed, along with short stories. She has published two collections: *Naming Dusk in Dead Languages* with Handstand Press, and *The Buoyancy of Space* with Grey Hen Press.

Maggie Norton was the South Cumbria Poet Laureate, in 2007. A Lancaster University prose and poetry tutor, she has five pamphlets and a collection published by Random, Scholastic, Pan Macmillan and BBC.

Meg Peacocke has lived several different lives, of which the most precarious, and the one that taught her most, was the quarter-century spent keeping a smallholding in east Cumbria. There, she was labourer, watcher, walker, writer and offcomer. Her book on the experience comes out in spring 2019. She was given a Cholmondeley Award 'for excellence in poetry' in 2005.

Mark G Pennington is a writer based in Kendal and is the author of *Barren Stories for Moonlit Mannequins,* (Dempsey & Windle 2018) his debut collection of poetry. He has recently been nominated for The Pushcart Prize and his poems have appeared in many magazines, journals and anthologies.

Tom Pickard was born in Newcastle upon Tyne and now lives in West Cumbria. His collected poems and songs, *hoyoot*, is published by Carcanet Press. *Winter Mirgants*, also published by Carcanet, won the Cumbria Life Writer of the year award. His latest book, *Fiends Fell*, a mix of prose and poetry in response to living in the Hartside Café for 10 years, was published in Chicago by Flood Editions and made the New York Times list of best ten (poetry) collections of 2017.

Chris Pilling was born in Birmingham but has lived in the Lake District for the past 40 years. He has published several books of his own poems and translations, mainly from French. In 2006, he was awarded the prestigious John Dryden prize for his translations of Catullus and is also an award-winning playwright.

Patricia Pogson moved to Staveley in Cumbria when she married the poet Geoffrey Holloway in 1977. She has lived there ever since, writing poetry, drawing, painting and messing about in her garden. She has produced six collections, been widely anthologised and won a few significant prizes.

Jacob Polley was born and grew up in Cumbria. He won the 2016 T.S. Eliot Prize for poetry for his fourth book of poems, *Jackself*. His first novel, *Talk of the Town* (2009), received the Somerset Maugham Award. Jacob is Professor of Creative Writing at Newcastle University and lives with his family on the North East coast.

Clare Proctor lives in the South Lakes where she works as an English teacher. She has had work published in the French Literary Review, Shooter, The North and on The Poetry Shed website, and is a member of Brewery Poets.

Solomon Russell-Cohen is a young writer. He is a student at Queen Elizabeth School in Kirkby Lonsdale and is a member of Dove Cottage Young Poets.

Eileen Pun is a Lake District based poet, devoted diarist, maker, fell-runner and has trained in martial arts for over twenty years. She has received a Northern Writers' Award and a Lisa Ullmann Travelling Scholarship in support of her interdisciplinary work in movement and poetry. She is published in national and international poetry anthologies, and has edited several books on Chinese culture and philosophy. www.eileenpun.com.

Maggie Reed (née How) now lives in West Malvern. She received an MA in Creative Writing from Lancaster University in 2015. Maggie has been published in The North magazine and Message in a Bottle, as well as numerous anthologies. She came third in Settle Sessions Poetry Competition in 2016.

Mary Robinson lived at Rosley in Cumbria from 1990 to 2017. She taught English literature in adult and higher education. Publications include, *The Art of Gardening* (Flambard Press, 2010); *Uist Waulking Song* (2012) and *Out of Time,* a poetry/photographic collaboration exhibited at Theatre-by-the-Lake in 2015. She won the Mirehouse Poetry Prize in 2013 and Second Light Poetry Prize in 2017. Her poetry is widely published in magazines and anthologies. maryrobinsonpoetry.blogspot.com.

David Scott, born 1947, was a parish priest in Cumbria in the 80s and has now retired to Kendal. He won the Sunday Times/BBC national poetry competition in 1978. His first book, *A Quiet Gathering,* won the Geoffrey Faber Memorial Prize; his second, *Playing for England,* a PBS recommendation

Jean Sly who was born in 1919, lived at Bandrake Head in South Cumbria from 1953 until her death in 2016. She taught English at Ulverston Grammar School and then infants at Lowick Green Primary School. After retirement, she was a school governor. Throughout her life she wrote poetry.

Mike Smith writes poetry, plays and essays (mostly on the short story form, in which he writes as Brindley Hallam Dennis). His writing has been published, broadcast and performed. He has lived in Cumbria since the day before his twenty-first birthday, and blogs at www.Bhdandme.wordpress.com.

Matt Sowerby is a member of Dove Cottage Young Poets and performs his poetry locally. His poem 'Breadlines' won the Poetry Society's End Hunger UK challenge for 16-18-year-olds. He is the 2018 Young Poet in Residence for Kendal Poetry Festival.

Jo Stoney is a serial multi-tasker, juggling writing with running two businesses and two jobs. Since moving to Cumbria in 1994, she has been a keen member of several writing groups, collaborative projects and an active member of Ulverston's Poem and a Pint group.

Alan John Stubbs is a prize winner in the Arvon International Poetry Competition. His first poetry collection, *the lost box of eyes* (2016), and his second collection, *ident*, were published by The Onslaught Press, who will also publish his third collection *tomorrow is the tugboat of today* in Autumn 2018.

Kathleen Swann grew up in the Lake District where her love of poetry and words was enhanced by brilliant English teachers. Now that she lives in Yorkshire, she writes out of doors and about the countryside and its characters as much as she can.

Hilary Tattershall is an off-comer, who has lived in Cockermouth for thirteen years, and can't imagine living anywhere else. On retiring from work she decided to give creativity free rein.

Hamish Wilson founded and directs The Garsdale Retreat in Cumbria. Formerly a drama teacher and playwright, he now writes and performs poetry. *Away from the Welsh Speaking Sea*, his illustrated sonnet sequence, was published in 2017, and in 2018 he was short-listed in the WoLF poetry competition.

Cathy Whittaker has fifteen poems published in Quintet (Cinnamon Press). Her poems have appeared in Under the Radar, Prole, The Interpreters House, Envoi, Orbis, Southlight, Mslexia, amongst others. She was shortlisted for the Bridport Prize. She has also been published in *#Me Too*: a women's poetry anthology edited by Debra Alma.

Pauline Yarwood is a poet and potter living in Cumbria. She is co-ordinator of Brewery Poets in Kendal and co-director of Kendal Poetry festival. Her debut pamphlet, *Image Junkie*, was published by Wayleave Press in 2017.

INDEX OF POETS